on track ...

The Temptations 1960-1978

every album, every song

George Haffenden

SONICBOND

sonicbondpublishing.com

Sonicbond Publishing Limited
www.sonicbondpublishing.co.uk
Email: info@sonicbondpublishing.co.uk

First Published in the United Kingdom 2025
First Published in the United States 2025

British Library Cataloguing in Publication Data:
A Catalogue record for this book is available from the British Library

ISBN 978-1-78952-373-7

Typeset in ITC Garamond Std & ITC Avant Garde Gothic
Printed and bound in England

Graphic design and typesetting: Full Moon Media

Follow us on social media:

Twitter: https://twitter.com/SonicbondP

Instagram: www.instagram.com/sonicbondpublishing_/

Facebook: www.facebook.com/SonicbondPublishing/

Linktree QR code:

Dedication

I'd like to thank Amy and Archie for tolerating me during the writing of this book and for listening along to every Temptations album released. I'd like to thank Stephen Lambe for allowing me to write the book and for his support.

Finally, I'd like to thank my parents for giving me this love of soul music, and especially my Dad, who took me to see The Temptations at the Royal Albert Hall in 2007 for the first time.

Would you like to write for Sonicbond Publishing?

We are mainly a music publisher, but we also occasionally publish in other genres including film and television. At Sonicbond Publishing we are always on the look-out for authors, particularly for our two main series, On Track and Decades.

Mixing fact with in depth analysis, the On Track series examines the entire recorded work of a particular musical artist or group. All genres are considered from easy listening and jazz to 60s soul to 90s pop, via rock and metal.

The Decades series singles out a particular decade in an artist or group's history and focuses on that decade in more detail than may be allowed in the On Track series.

While professional writing experience would, of course, be an advantage, the most important qualification is to have real enthusiasm and knowledge of your subject. First-time authors are welcomed, but the ability to write well in English is essential.

Sonicbond Publishing has distribution throughout Europe and North America, and all our books are also published in E-book form. Authors will be paid a royalty based on sales of their book. Further details about our books are available from www.sonicbondpublishing.com. To contact us, complete the contact form there or email info@sonicbondpublishing.co.uk *on track ...*

The Temptations

1960-1978

Contents

Introduction 7
Meet The Temptations (1964) 15
The Temptations Sing Smokey (1965) 24
The Temptin' Temptations (1965) 35
Gettin' Ready (1966) 43
With A Lot O' Soul (1967) 52
In A Mellow Mood (1967) 60
The Temptations Wish It Would Rain (1968) 67
Cloud Nine (1969) 74
Puzzle People (1969) 85
Psychedelic Shack (1970) 93
Sky's The Limit (1971) 99
Solid Rock (1972) 106
All Directions (1972) 116
Masterpiece (1973) 123
1990 (1973) 129
A Song For You (1975) 138
House Party (1975) 144
Wings Of Love (1976) 149
Do The Temptations (1976) 153
Here To Tempt You (1977) 158
Bare Back (1978) 164
Other Albums 170
Live Albums 173
Epilogue 176

Introduction

> The Tempts epitomised tall, dark and handsome, standing over six feet, each a distinctive personality … Up on that stage were five stars, each of whom could have been a lead singer.
> Berry Gordy

> All stories have heroes, and ours are the generations of Temptations who made up the group. Every whirl, every step, every wave of our hands, took five guys, in harmony, in step, in style, on a journey of a lifetime.
> Otis Williams

There can be few groups who have, directly or indirectly, not been influenced by The Temptations. One of the greatest singing groups of all time, their name alone conjures up a certain class; their incredible harmonies, excellent lead singers and sharp choreography all combined to create a trailblazing way of performing. In their peak, few groups could match The Temptations for both style and popularity, and today, their legacy as soul music's finest is assured.

Formed in Detroit from two local groups, The Distants and The Primes, the group first auditioned for Motown founder Berry Gordy Jr in 1961. Gordy was the product of a hard-working black family who were pillars of the local community, owning businesses and prominent in local politics. Unlike his siblings – Gordy was the second youngest of eight – he took his time to find his calling. Always drawn to music, he co-wrote several songs for Jackie Wilson, including 'Reet Petite' and 'Lonely Teardrops', but was dismayed by his lack of financial reward. He also opened (and closed) a failed jazz record shop, attempted door-to-door sales and also spent time working at the Ford automobile factory on the assembly line. It was here that he developed his concept for Motown: a musical assembly line that took raw talent from Detroit's streets, polished them up, gave them hits, in turn making them national and international stars.

After discovering The Miracles in 1957 and befriending their lead singer, William 'Smokey' Robinson, Gordy, encouraged by Robinson, borrowed $600 from his family's mutual investment fund, set up his new venture at 2468 West Grand Boulevard and boldly nicknamed it 'Hitsville USA'. The label eventually became a symbol of black capitalism and upward mobility, creating music that transcended the racial barrier on a global scale.

When The Temptations first auditioned for Gordy, they called themselves 'The Elgins'. They consisted of Otis Williams, Melvin Franklin and Eldridge 'Al' Byrant from The Distants, and Paul Williams and Eddie Kendricks from The Primes (The Primes also had a female equivalent, The Primettes, who soon morphed into The Supremes and also joined Motown). Both groups had sung locally, with Otis Williams, in particular, being a serial leader of singing groups around Detroit, and even had The Distants signed with a manager and recorded a minor hit called 'Come On 'in 1960. But as The Distants floundered, the merger with The Primes made sense, especially given the incredible voices that both Eddie Kendricks and Paul Williams possessed. Both could sing lead and harmonise, and Paul had a flair for choreography, setting the new group apart from other singing groups, who simply stood next to their microphones. Gordy was impressed enough to sign them, but told them they needed a new name. The Elgins was already taken.

According to Otis Williams in his autobiography, it was he who came up with the name 'Temptations', writing later that 'we knew we weren't going to tempt anyone or anything, but, what the hell, it was as good a name as any'. Paul Williams, though, thought 'Maybe it will give us something to live up to.'

Success took a while to achieve, though. Their initial recordings showed promise but failed to light up the charts. Frustrated with a lack of success, Al Bryant began lashing out at the other members and was eventually fired from the group after an altercation with Paul Williams in which Bryant smashed him over the head with a glass bottle. It was a rash decision that he'd surely come to regret as the group hired, as his replacement, David Ruffin, a powerful, gospel-infused shouter whose voice would transform The Temptations' sound. Ruffin had the determination and talent to match, with plenty of vocal firepower and charisma, which would make the group, but would also nearly destroy it.

This became known as the 'Classic Five' lineup, the one which most fans associate with the name 'The Temptations', and the one that yielded most of their classic hits. Almost immediately after Ruffin's hiring, the group had their first big hit, the Smokey Robinson-penned and produced 'The Way You Do The Things You Do'. From there on, Robinson continued to produce a number of hits for the group, from 'Since I Lost My Baby' to 'It's Growing' to perhaps his most famous composition, 'My Girl', Ruffin's first lead as a Temptation.

Unlike most groups of the time, The Temptations were unique in having multiple members of the group singing lead on different songs. In their pre-Ruffin days, the leads were split between Paul Williams and Eddie Kendricks, and naturally, once Ruffin joined the fold, he, too, sang lead. Motown's PR machine, therefore, dubbed them the group with 'five lead singers', however rare it was for Otis Williams or Melvin Franklin to sing lead.

Given their talent, other producers at Motown also wanted the chance to record with them, primarily Norman Whitfield, who joined the company early on and impressed Gordy with his persistence, doing whatever jobs were necessary to get his songs cut. He joined Motown's famed 'Quality Control' department, which ensured all single releases had hit potential, before beginning to write songs, contributing to early Marvin Gaye hits like 'Pride & Joy'. He went on to be one of Motown's most crucial writers and producers, but it was his work with The Temptations that was his best and most important. His first hit single for them was 1966's 'Ain't Too Proud Beg' and was only released after Smokey Robinson's effort, 'Get Ready', stalled on the pop charts. His success ensured that he would become The Temptations' main producer for the next seven years, steering the group away from the softer, melodic tracks of Smokey Robinson into harder-hitting soul and funk, both in terms of sound and lyrical content.

Behind the scenes, the pressures of fame led to greater temptations that proved difficult to resist: Paul Williams, who already had health problems, began drinking heavily, while David Ruffin indulged in women and drugs, his ego inflating daily. Kendricks, meanwhile, who was always a bit of a loner, eventually drifted away from the rest of the group and harboured ambitions to go solo.

However, Ruffin was the first to leave The Temptations. Seeing how other Motown acts were now being promoted, such as Diana Ross & The Supremes and Smokey Robinson & The Miracles, he wanted the same for himself, suggesting they now be known as 'David Ruffin & The Temptations'. While Ruffin sang the bulk of the leads, Kendricks and Paul Williams also did, meaning this was a non-starter. His behaviour also became more erratic, and the situation came to a head in 1968 when the others voted Ruffin out of the group.

His replacement was Dennis Edwards, another gospel-shouter, who could handle the Ruffin-era songs while injecting an intensity of his own into the lineup. His arrival marked a shift in the group's sound, as Whitfield drew inspiration from the new 'psychedelic soul' pioneered by Sly & The Family Stone and gave The Temptations and Motown their first Grammy-winning song, 'Cloud Nine'. It was both musically and lyrically creative by Motown's standards, but its less-than-subtle drug references initially worried Gordy. Nevertheless, its chart success heralded in a new era of message songs for both The Temptations and Motown.

This second-greatest Temptations lineup only lasted until 1971, but in that period, the group continued to have big hits, from the funk of 'I Can't Get Next To You' to the haunting majesty of 'Just My Imagination (Running Away With Me)'. But illness and tensions within the group continued to take their toll, and by 1972, only Otis Williams and Melvin Franklin remained as the group's original members. Hits would continue, but they would rarely be as big as those that went before, and as the 1970s closed, the group struggled in the unforgiving world of disco, culminating in their own attempts to embrace the genre in the late 1970s.

This book charts The Temptations' albums from 1964 to 1978, covering their first 20 albums. During this period, though, the years 1965 to 1972 were their most successful commercially and critically. Other members would leave and join, and, in 1976, the group decided to leave Motown Records, signing with Atlantic Records in an attempt to boost their flagging careers. Frustratingly, though, the two albums they released while signed to Atlantic sold poorly and failed to spark a creative resurgence for the group. With the release of the second album, *Bare Back*, Atlantic and The Temptations parted ways, leaving the group with an uncertain future.

A Note On Sources

The only memoir from one of the 'Classic Five' Temptations is Otis Williams', first published in 1988 and subsequently re-published with a chapter in 2002, and reissued as an audiobook with a new section in 2020. Likewise, the majority of interviews with The Temptations have been led by Williams, and to a lesser degree, Melvin Franklin. Former members have attested to Williams' leadership of the group, including taking the leading role in interviews, so much of The Temptations' story is from the perspective of Williams.

However, Mark Ribowsky's excellent biography of the group features interviews with former members, and former member Richard Street was in the process of writing his own memoir before he died in 2013. His conversations with writer Toi Moore were turned into a book, *My Life As A Temptation*, released after his death, in which he criticised Williams' handling of the group, and his own treatment as a member.

Above: The 'Classic Five' Temptations in white in 1964. (*Motown*)

Left: The Temptations' debut album (1964), featuring their latest recruit, David Ruffin. (*Gordy/Motown*)

Right: *Sing Smokey* (1965) contains songs written and produced by William 'Smokey' Robinson, then Motown's biggest male star. (*Gordy/Motown*)

Left: *The Temptin' Temptations* (1965) saw the arrival of Norman Whitfield as a producer for The Temptations. (*Gordy/Motown*)

Right: *Gettin' Ready* (1966) marked a transition from Robinson to Whitfield as the group's primary producer. (*Gordy/Motown*)

Left: By 1967 and the release of *With A Lot O' Soul*, The Temptations had become one of Motown's prime acts. (*Gordy/Motown*)

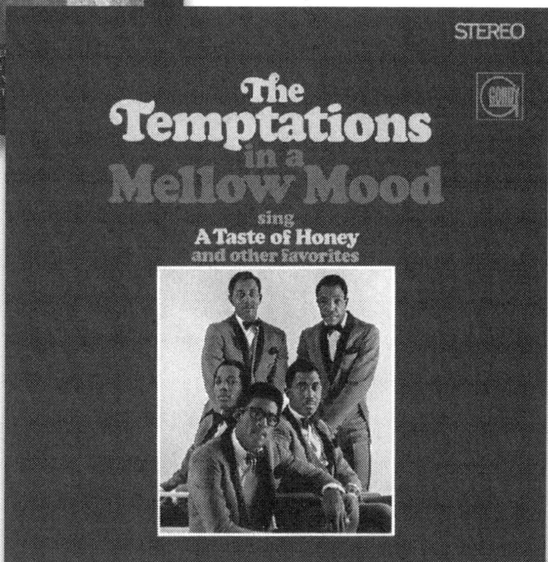

Right: The cover of *In A Mellow Mood* (1967) shows The Temptations at their most sophisticated, singing the Great American Songbook. (*Gordy/Motown*)

Left: The 'Classic Five' lineup of Paul Williams, Eddie Kendricks, David Ruffin, Otis Williams and Melvin Franklin in 1964. (*James Kriegsmann*)

Below: Smokey Robinson, in striped bathrobe, rehearsing 'My Girl' with the group backstage at the Apollo Theater, New York City, in 1964. (*Don Paulsen/Michael Ochs Archives/Getty*)

Meet The Temptations (1964)

Personnel:
Otis Williams, Melvin Franklin, Paul Williams, Eddie Kendricks, Eldridge 'Al' Bryant, David Ruffin (on 'The Way You Do The Things You Do' only): vocals
The Funk Brothers: instrumentation
Produced at Hitsville USA, Detroit, by Berry Gordy, Andre Williams, William 'Mickey' Stevenson, Smokey Robinson and Norman Whitfield between October 1963 and January 1964
Label: Gordy
Release date: 13 April 1964
Length: 31:33
Chart position: US pop: 95

After signing with Motown in 1961, The Temptations initially struggled to reach a level of success that would merit an album release. Berry Gordy himself had written and produced several singles for the group, but with little success. Eventually, Smokey Robinson, in between writing, producing and touring with his group The Miracles, gave the group their first national hit, the evergreen single 'The Way You Do The Things You Do'. Released in January 1964, Motown decided that it was now worthwhile releasing an album by the group, capitalising on their newfound fame, and it would be titled, appropriately, *Meet The Temptations*. It was hardly an original title, for The Supremes had released their own *Meet The Supremes* album in December 1962, and the concept was the same: introduce the group to a wider audience by collecting their previous singles on an album. It also made financial sense: no new material was needed, so no additional recording costs were incurred.

In this early period, as the tracks on *Meet The Temptations* show, the group were recorded by almost anyone who wanted them, including Gordy himself, A&R man William 'Mickey' Stevenson and Norman Whitfield. They even recorded two songs with Clarence Paul, who would shepherd Stevie Wonder's early career, as 'The Pirates' on Motown's short-lived imprint label 'Melody' (these songs weren't included on *Meet The Temptations*, however, but are now available on *50th Anniversary: The Singles Collection 1961-1971*). Otis Williams recalled that Gordy joked that if 'The Pirates' singles had been successful, the group would spend the rest of their days performing in pirate outfits.' He wrote that they would 'have died for a hit, but if it meant going through life in pirate uniforms, no thanks.' Luckily for the group, the singles weren't hits, and their time as 'The Pirates' was blissfully short.

As Williams recalled, Motown was a singles-driven company; therefore, their approach to albums could be summarised in the following way:

> Basically, selling an album was like reselling one, two or three hit singles, plus some throwaway filler tracks that nobody really gave a damn about.

Interestingly, unlike some of the earlier Motown album covers, which featured cartoons or often white faces (*Come And Get These Memories* by Martha Reeves & The Vandellas had a teddy bear on the front, while Mary Wells's *The One Who Really Loves You* had cartoon love-hearts), *Meet The Temptations* featured the new, soon-to-be 'Classic Five' lineup on the front, posing against a dark background, looking contemplative with all but David Ruffin (not yet wearing his trademark spectacles) staring directly at the camera, exuding class and confidence.

Equally interesting here is that several of the group are given writing credits: famously, Gordy largely compartmentalised Motown along the lines of Detroit's automobile factories, having separate departments to handle different areas of the business, rarely allowing a member of staff to straddle several parts, unless, of course, your name was Smokey Robinson. Yet, on *Meet The Temptations,* with the exception of Paul Williams, all the group members contribute writing, something that, later on during their time at Motown, Williams claims they were prevented from doing.

Eldridge 'Al' Bryant appears on all the tracks apart from 'The Way You Do The Things You Do'. After the group's initial lack of success, Bryant grew frustrated and restless, and after an altercation backstage following a performance when Bryant wanted to give the crowd another encore but the rest declined, he flipped and ended up glassing Paul Williams with a bottle of beer, requiring hospitalisation. The others, naturally, wanted Bryant fired immediately, but, trying to keep the peace, Paul stepped in for him and the inevitable was put off for a couple of months. During the Motown Christmas party, Bryant's attitude so disturbed Otis Williams that when he suggested letting Bryant go, the others agreed. Bryant was out, and David Ruffin was in.

Ruffin's timing was perfect, joining the group just weeks before Robinson presented them with 'The Way You Do The Things You Do', their first hit, which still endures today and remains part of the group's core live repertoire. This, along with Ruffin's arrival, marked a welcome change in fortunes for the group.

After nearly three years struggling at Motown while others like The Miracles and Mary Wells were having national success (they even backed Wells on tour, compounding the humiliation), The Temptations were simply thrilled, with Otis Williams recalling:

> We'd prayed for that album for so long – we cherished it. Each one of us had his own copy, and when we were on the road and staying someplace, walking down the hall, we'd hear it playing.

Along with the recordings made as 'The Pirates', two earlier singles – 'Oh Mother Of Mine' and 'Romance Without Finance'– were also not included, both produced by Stevenson and Andre Williams. They were later included on the 1999 CD reissue.

Meet The Temptations holds up well listening back today. It shows the faith that Gordy, Robinson, Stevenson and others at Motown had in the group's abilities, even as their initial run of singles flopped. Looking back six decades later, it's clear the album is a pivotal moment in the group's history, where both Motown and The Temptations hadn't quite found their signature sound, although there's plenty to suggest the greatness to come. It also allowed Motown to market The Temptations as the hottest new act from Hitsville USA, even if the group had been signed three years earlier.

'The Way You Do The Things You Do' (Smokey Robinson, Bobby Rodgers)

A week after David Ruffin joined the group, Smokey Robinson let the group know he'd booked the studio to record a new song he'd written, a song that would transform the group's fortune and become their first major hit. Robinson had co-written the song while driving back from a performance with The Miracles, along with his bandmate Bobby Rodgers. The song had a jaunty feel, with some typically sweet Robinson lyrics bordering on the corny. For example:

> You got a smile so bright
> You know you could've been a candle
> I'm holding you so tight
> You know you could've been a handle
> The way you swept me off my feet
> You know you could've been a broom
> And baby you smell so sweet
> You know you could've been some perfume

Yet, somehow, Robinson made the song work. He gave the lead to Kendricks, who sings in his exceptionally clear falsetto throughout, the sweetness of his voice mirroring that of Robinson's lyrics. The backing harmonies are equally sweet, especially as the song comes to a close, repeating the song's title as Kendricks sings to the woman in the song about all the things she does to him. The group are backed by The Funk Brothers, Motown's in-house backing band that performed on the majority of the label's recordings from 1959 until 1972 when the company relocated to California. One of the guitarists, Eddie Willis, plays the riff at the centre of the track and James Jamerson's light, bouncy bass, along with a funky horn arrangement. There's a bonus saxophone solo from Henry Cosby, which, on stage, gave the chance for the group to show off their trademark choreography.

Otis Williams recalled in his autobiography:

> The first time we heard the song, we loved it. The melody swung, and the lyrics had lots of charm. They were silly in a way, talking about a girl you

> loved as a candle, a handle, a schoolbook, a cool crook, a broom, a perfume, but, typical of Smokey, he made it work.

In time, Williams would come to understand the lyrics as a parody of what guys tell girls as they're trying to seduce, and after the group's initial reservations over the words, they began to love the song. The record-buying public, too, valued the song, buying enough copies of the single to give The Temptations their first national hit, reaching an impressive number 11 on the US pop charts. The group only found out about its success when they returned to Detroit after another gruelling 'Motortown Revue' tour. Ruffin was so overwhelmed by the news that he broke down in tears. As Williams would write, 'there would be bigger hits, but nothing ever beat that first time'.

With the success of Kendricks fronting the group here, the next two Temptations singles would also feature him on lead vocals, the excellent (although less well-selling) 'I'll Be In Trouble' and 'Girl (Why You Wanna Make Me Blue)'. Both these songs would be included on their third album, *The Temptin' Temptations*.

'I Want A Love I Can See' (Smokey Robinson)
'The Way You Do The Things You Do' might have given the group their first hit with Smokey Robinson, but it was 'I Want A Love I Can See' that was their first collaboration on an A-side single release. While certainly not as polished as 'The Way You Do The Things You Do' or later Robinson-penned hits, 'I Want A Love I Can See' certainly pointed the group in the direction for what was to come: cute lyrics, tight grooves laid down by the Funk Brothers and excellent lead and background vocals.

Paul Williams was given the lead by Robinson, figuring it suited his deeper baritone the best; at this point, Ruffin had yet to join the group, and so Williams split most of the lead vocals with Kendricks. Williams was later overlooked by Motown producers in favour of Ruffin, Kendricks and eventually Dennis Edwards, but his emotive baritone is exquisite: it's not quite the gospel-infused shouting of Ruffin or Edwards, but his bluesy tone suited the slower tempos. That certainly worked well on 'I Want A Love I Can See', a song ostensibly about what the narrator wants in a woman; with Paul Williams on the lead, it becomes more melancholy.

The song is driven by the piano playing and some jazz-influenced drumming, with a punchy horn arrangement in the choruses. It's not as sophisticated as later Motown hits, but it's certainly enjoyable, thanks largely to the brilliant lead from Williams and the lively backing vocals that, in parts, echo Williams' lines. They're suitably tight and smooth, repeating the line 'don'tcha know I want a love?' in the choruses and as the song fades out.

Despite the quality of the song, when released as a single in March 1968, it didn't chart nationally, although it became a part of their live act and was released on the *Recorded Live At The Motortown Revue* album in 1964 and was also included as part of the opening medley on their own *Temptations Live* album in 1966. The group later revisited the song on their 2001 album *Awesome*, this time with Otis Williams as the last original member of the group and sung by later-era member Terry Weeks.

'(You're My) Dream Come True' (Berry Gordy Jr)
Robinson might have had the first hit by the group, but it was Gordy who ran most of the early sessions for The Temptations, his faith so great in the group and their unique vocal blend that he wrote and produced most of the tracks that ended up on *Meet The Temptations*. 'Dream Come True' might be the best of his writing efforts for the group, a beautiful ballad that, acting up to its title, has a dreamy sound and feel.

Gordy's then-wife, Raynoma, plays harpsichord on the track, helping to achieve that dream-like feeling. Raynoma was a key individual in the early days of Motown, yet her contribution is often overlooked today. She first auditioned as a singer for Gordy, but he was more impressed with her writing and arranging abilities. Along with Smokey Robinson, Raynoma encouraged Gordy to start his own label and she took charge of their publishing arm, Jobete. Their marriage didn't last long, though, thanks to Gordy's numerous affairs.

Given the song's soft nature, it's no surprise that Gordy chose Kendricks to sing the lead; his smooth, almost heavenly, tenor vocals reflect the dreamy quality of the arrangement. The rest of the group, meanwhile, provide doo-wop influenced backing vocals.

It was the second single to be released by the group, after 'Oh, Mother Of Mine', and hit a decent number 22 on the US R&B charts, the only single to chart before the release of 'The Way You Do The Things You Do'.

'Paradise' (Berry Gordy Jr)
From the opening beat, you'd be forgiven for thinking this was a Frankie Valli & The Four Seasons track, sounding remarkably similar to their 1962 hit 'Sherry'. The beat and groove are almost identical; Williams confirms in his autobiography that Gordy had written it in the 'Sherry' mould, and again, given Valli's own impressive falsetto, it made sense to give the lead vocal to Kendricks. He delivers a lovely vocal, with Franklin providing the bass 'boom-booms' throughout the track, while the other Temptations harmonise sweetly.

It was the follow-up single to 'Dream Come True', released in September 1962, but this time, it didn't chart on either the R&B or pop charts. Williams later wrote that they 'later heard that it was a regional success in parts of California, but that was all.'

'May I Have This Dance' (Janie Bradford, Norman Whitfield)
According to Williams, this marked the first time Whitfield wrote and produced The Temptations. It was released as the B-side to the single

'Farewell, My Love' and features Kendricks on lead, but not in his normal falsetto; he sings the bulk of the song in a lower register, sounding less comfortable than he does on the rest of his early leads in his usual falsetto. It's an intriguing choice and one that wouldn't be repeated. Whitfield was clearly attempting to try something new with The Temptations, but on all subsequent songs that featured Kendricks as the lead singer, he used his falsetto. Musically, it's also very much anchored by doo-wop influences, especially the backing vocals, in which Paul Williams is the most audible.

Lyrically, it packs a lot in the couple of minutes the song lasts: the narrator is shy and fears asking the girl he likes to dance before she dances with another guy, who he can't compete against, so he schemes to convince the guy that another girl, Pearl, is waiting for him. Not quite the 'Keep It Simple, Stupid' mantra Gordy would later enforce, it's nonetheless a typical theme for the era, where a boy meets a girl he admires but can't seem to get her.

It was a start for Whitfield producing The Temptations, but it certainly didn't anticipate what they were to achieve together later in the decade.

'Isn't She Pretty' (Berry Gordy Jr, Eddie Kendricks, Otis Williams)
Written in collaboration between Gordy, Kendricks and Williams, 'Isn't She Pretty' is a fast-paced doo-wop number, not dissimilar to Williams' early regional hit, 'Come On', with The Distants. The tempo is more frantic here, and the lead, like many of their later songs, is split among the group. They begin singing the first verse in unison, with Franklin providing more doo-wop style 'boom-booms', before Paul Williams and Al Bryant sing the second and third verse, with Kendricks and Franklin pairing up in the bridge, and Otis Williams also getting a line to sing. That type of lead splitting would remerge later on, notably when Whitfield took over as the group's main producer. It would end up on the flip side of the single 'Dream Come True'.

'Just Let Me Know' (Berry Gordy Jr)
Another Gordy production, this time with Paul Williams providing the lead vocal, 'Just Let Me Know' is another pleading, mid-tempo breakup song in which Williams, as the narrator, sings to the girl who left him. Not giving up, though, Williams is ready to 'come running back, as fast as I can' to her if she just lets him know she's interested in him, too. It's one of the stronger Gordy compositions for the group, featuring some excellent guitar and loud organ playing, driving things along and making the song sound happier than the lyrics suggest it should be.

'Your Wonderful Love' (Berry Gordy Jr)
Perhaps the best song Gordy wrote for the group, 'Your Wonderful Love' is a beautifully soft ballad in which the song's narrator, again Paul Williams singing the lead, declares his unending love for his girl, declaring 'I'm so

happy, when I can tell my friends you're my girl' thanks to her 'wonderful love'. Its straightforward lyrics, perhaps bordering on the schmaltzy, are delivered with such passion and force by Williams, masking any deficiencies in Gordy's writing. Otis Williams later recalled that 'Your Wonderful Love' reminded him of The Impressions' later hit 'For Your Precious Love', written by Curtis Mayfield. Indeed, both songs communicate similar expressions of love and both feature baritone leads, with Jerry Butler singing the lead for The Impressions.

Despite its strength, it was released as the B-side to 'Check Yourself', the group's second single, in November 1961. Neither side, however, charted.

'The Further You Look, the Less You See' (Smokey Robinson, Norman Whitfield)

Co-written by Norman Whitfield, but produced by Smokey Robinson, Williams notes in his autobiography that it was one of the first songs that Whitfield contributed to the group. Perhaps Robinson saw his role as mentoring the newcomer Whitfield here, but whatever the situation, it's a beautiful track that points more in the direction that the group, and Motown more generally, would take, with less reliance on doo-wop influences and more emphasis on powerful, emotive lead vocals and more creative backing vocals. It features a smooth groove, with some incredibly tight vocals – even at this early juncture, the years performing locally had honed the group's vocal chops almost to perfection.

Paul Williams is again given the lead, and he delivers yet another gut-wrenching performance, his baritone strong and emotional, as he sings about a girl he wants, warning her that the more she looks for a man, the less she'll find – suggesting that she's best off choosing the narrator. Williams sums this up with the line, 'I'm hoping you'd be the treasure meant for me'.

It was released as the B-side to the single release of 'I Want A Love I Can See', relegated to the group's long history.

'Check Yourself' (Eldridge Bryant, Melvin Franklin, Berry Gordy, Otis Williams)

According to Otis Williams, writing 'Check Yourself' was a collaborative effort, although, in his memoirs, he took credit for writing the bulk of the song. After singing it to A&R head Mickey Stevenson, he helped the group put the song together before playing a rough cut to Gordy, who was equally impressed. The song also made its way past Brian Holland, of the famed Holland-Dozier-Holland writing trio, who suggested some changes to the bridge. The result, according to Williams, was a much better single, saying that, at that time, 'Hitsville was like a hit record think-tank. Anyone's two cents were welcome.' Oddly, though, only Gordy shares in the writing credit; others from the early days of Motown have claimed that Gordy would award writing credits for himself, even if his input was minimal.

Otis Williams begins the song, which starts with a bluesy, moody arrangement, and his vocal is mirrored by Franklin before Paul Williams takes the lead when the tempo shifts around the 30-second mark, becoming an uptempo, almost dance number. The fast tempo, like so many Motown hits, masks the sadness of the lyrics, as Paul Williams sings about a lost love and how sorrowful he is, warning his fellow man to 'check yourself' and avoid his sad, lonely fate. It's an impassioned vocal from Paul Williams, who, at this point, was still nominally the group's lead singer.

Yet, 'Check Yourself' wasn't a hit nationally and failed to chart when released as a single in November 1961.

'Slow Down Heart' (Smokey Robinson)

Another early lost gem from Robinson, 'Slow Down Heart' is a combination of doo-wop vocals, an R&B groove and an almost Latin-jazz beat, upon which the group demonstrate their finely tuned harmonies. Paul Williams sings the lead again, and the backing vocals are dominated by Kendricks and Franklin: Kendricks sings the harmonies incredibly sweetly, while Franklin's bass vocal grounds the rest of the harmonies.

The drumming is repetitive throughout, sounding almost like a military band, albeit one with a rhythm section. Robinson adds a flute and saxophone solo about halfway through, though both are mixed softly into the background while The Temptations intersperse with repeated yells of 'Hey!'

Not deemed strong enough to be an A-side, it was originally released on the B-side of Gordy's production 'Farewell, My Love'.

'Farewell, My Love' (Berry Gordy)

Another Gordy composition and production, the harmonies on 'Farewell, My Love' are simply exquisite. The song is essentially the second part (or perhaps the first part) of 'Slow Down Heart' with a similar narrative. The song opens with the group harmonising the line 'farewell my love', singing the first verse in unison, with Franklin providing even more 'boom-booms' throughout, before Paul Williams and Kendricks share the rest of the lead. Paul Williams also provides a spoken-word verse, addressing the girl in the song, bidding her adieu.

Lyrically, it's not as strong as others on *Meet The Temptations*, being far less catchy, but the harmonies rescue the song as much as possible – although the ending sounds a little dated, like something the vocal harmony group The Four Freshmen might have done a decade earlier, with their barbershop-quartet style. It finishes with a brief moment of acappella harmonising before the song ends; the harmonies, like those of the Freshman, are incredibly rich but lack an R&B edge. Yet, two decades later, Otis Williams wrote in his memoirs:

> 'Farewell My Love' is worth hearing today because it features Paul and Eddie Kendricks on the lead. Paul did most leads then, and Al left us before our

big hits, so his singing is not as familiar to the public as it deserves to be. He was a floating tenor, which meant his voice could roam all around up there, then blend back in with the harmony. It was something to hear him. When he'd come in with one of those parts onstage, it drove people nuts.

1999 CD Reissue Bonus Tracks

'Oh, Mother Of Mine' (William 'Mickey' Stevenson)
It's hard to know why Gordy and Motown didn't include 'Oh, Mother Of Mine' on *Meet The Temptations*; perhaps Gordy, selfishly, wanted his songs to take priority and boost his own royalties. But 'Oh, Mother Of Mine' is an early Motown stomper, featuring an excellent split vocal between Paul Williams and Eddie Kendricks. It was the group's first single release after signing with Motown, released on the short-lived Miracle imprint. It failed to chart upon its release, perhaps reflecting both the group's limited national recognition at the time and Motown's own promotional issues as a then-small independent label. It was later included on the group's five-CD career retrospective *Emperors Of Soul* in 1994.

'Romance Without Finance' (William 'Mickey' Stevenson, Eddie Kendricks)
Possibly the most forgettable early track by The Temptations is this, an odd-sounding attempt at hard-hitting R&B, dominated by some loud piano bashing and an admittedly nice guitar riff. Yet, its frantic pace makes it hard for Paul Williams to be heard in parts and for him to even keep up with the instrumentation. This was the flip to the single release of 'Oh, Mother Of Mine', a track Otis Williams could barely recall, and it featured neither on *Meet The Temptations* nor as part of the group's live act.

The Temptations Sing Smokey (1965)

Personnel:
Otis Williams, Melvin Franklin, Paul Williams, Eddie Kendricks, David Ruffin, Eldridge 'Al' Bryant (on 'Baby, Baby I Need You' only): vocals
The Funk Brothers: instrumentation
Produced at Hitsville USA, Detroit, by William 'Smokey' Robinson
Recording dates: September 1963 to March 1965
Label: Gordy
Release date: 12 March 1965
Length: 33:49
Chart: US pop: 35, US R&B: 1

The second Temptations album, *Sing Smokey*, was released in the wake of the release and success of 'My Girl', a Smokey Robinson-penned hit that gave the group their first number-one pop hit. With David Ruffin in the group, Robinson had a new muse to write for, one who could interpret his lyrics and deliver unbelievably brilliant lead vocals. And, given Robinson's own success as the lead singer of The Miracles, Motown's top male act at the time, using his image to promote The Temptations no doubt made commercial sense.

Berry Gordy himself even wrote the notes for the album, writing that the collaboration between Robinson and The Temptations had...

> ...[I]nevitably produced results which have given me, and our entire organisation, great pride in our association with them. It has also, I am sure, given you the same enjoyment.

Yet, being a singles driven company, Motown didn't bother getting Robinson to write any further tracks in the wake of 'My Girl' to complete the album, instead packing it with older songs left in the Motown vaults, such as 'Baby, Baby I Need You', recorded before 'My Girl' and even before Ruffin joined the group, featuring Al Bryant, not Ruffin, on the harmonies. The songs were recorded over a nearly two-year period, the last being completed in early 1965.

The theme of the album, obvious given the title, was to have the group sing only Smokey Robinson-penned songs. This explains the exclusion of two earlier, non-Robinson-produced singles, 'I'll Be In Trouble' and 'Girl (Why You Wanna Make Me Blue)', written by Norman Whitfield and Eddie Holland. Both tracks later appeared on their third album, *The Temptin' Temptations*, despite both being released before 'My Girl'. However, given the success of 'My Girl', it perhaps made business sense to hold onto these singles to bulk out a future Temptations album.

Indeed, *Sing Smokey* highlights Motown's early approach to albums: a few hit singles, filler tracks that didn't have the potential to be singles and plenty of covers. It also introduced the group to the concept of Motown acts covering each other's songs. This meant that Motown, through its publishing arm, Jobete, which controlled its publishing, could keep publishing fees and royalties in-house, rather than paying another publisher to cover songs they controlled. As a result, if one act had a hit, you could bet that another Motown act would cover it for a forthcoming album as 'filler'. Here, plenty of songs are recycled for The Temptations, including several early Motown classics, such as 'You Beat Me To The Punch' (originally by Mary Wells) and The Miracles' 'You Really Got A Hold On Me', and this would be common practice on future albums, too.

Despite this, in his autobiography, Williams claimed that compared with *Meet The Temptations*, both *Sing Smokey* and the follow-up, *The Temptin' Temptations,* 'more thought went into the filler tracks, and so these records still hold up today.' Certainly, the production quality is better than their first effort and the vocals are more polished. The leads are split between newcomer Ruffin, Kendricks and Paul Williams, although Williams would soon find himself with fewer leads on future single releases and albums supplanted by Ruffin. Here, though, when called upon, Williams delivers some excellent vocals.

In the end, *Sing Smokey* was a big success for the group, reaching number 35 on the US pop charts and hitting number one on the R&B album charts (which had only begun in January 1965, which explains why *Meet The Temptations* only hit the pop charts).

'The Way You Do The Things You Do' (Smokey Robinson, Bobby Rogers)

Given the song's popularity and importance to the group, it was included again on *Sing Smokey* after already appearing on *Meet The Temptations*. Naturally, it also meant no additional song was required to fill the album and guaranteed additional fees for Motown's publishing company Jobete.

'Baby, Baby I Need You' (Smokey Robinson)

Recorded in 1963, 'Baby, Baby I Need You' features some excellent harmonising by the group as they sing most of the lead in unison, although, in parts, Paul Williams and Eddie Kendricks trade the lead. The song doesn't feature Ruffin in the harmonies, being recorded before he joined the group, and as a result, this was the last song to be released featuring Al Bryant. It highlights Motown's approaches to albums in this period: why bother recording the song again, as it was only essentially filler on *Sing Smokey?*

A beautiful, slow ballad, it sounds less evergreen than something like 'My Girl'. Similar to their earlier songs on *Meet The Temptations*, the vocals are in the style of 1950s doo-wop ballads, with a slight hint of gospel when the group sing all at once. The instrumentation is bluesy and is dominated by the saxophone and organ, but it's less striking than the joyous arrangement Robinson gives to 'My Girl'. Nevertheless, the vocals are exquisite and were a part of the group's live set for several years; a version was recorded for their first live album, *Temptations Live!*, in 1966. It was also released as the B-side to the group's single 'Girl (Why You Wanna Make Me Blue)' in 1964.

'My Girl' (Smokey Robinson, Ronald White)
With the arrival of David Ruffin in the group, The Temptations now had an outstanding lead vocalist whom Smokey Robinson could write for. In an interview with *NPR*, Robinson said:

> David Ruffin, I knew, was like this sleeping giant in this group because he had this mellow, gruff-sounding voice. And all I needed was the right song for his voice, and I felt like I would have a smash hit record. So, I sat down at the piano to write a song for David Ruffin's voice. I wanted to make it something that he could belt out, yet make it melodic and sweet.

According to Williams, the song was originally due to be cut by The Miracles, but, as Robinson wrote in his memoirs, 'I saw David back there, waiting to explode', and decided it would suit Ruffin's voice better. It would be his first lead vocal on a Temptations single.

Robinson introduced the group to the song between appearances at the famed Apollo Theatre in Harlem before recording it back in Detroit. While Robinson coached Ruffin, working out the melody and how he should sing it, he left the background vocals to the others, later recalling:

> I always let The Temptations make up their own background vocals because they were always so great at doing their own background vocals. They could all sing so well.

As a result, the backing vocals respond to Ruffin's lead, echoing and repeating 'my girl' twice in the chorus; Paul Williams sings first before the rest fall in for the second repetition, adding to the catchiness of the chorus, and, importantly, making the song a group effort rather than simply just a vehicle for Ruffin.

The song opens with James Jameson's bass guitar repeating the 'bah-bum-bum' pattern before Robert White plays the catchy guitar riff that repeats throughout the song. The Funk Brothers provide the rhythm track as normal and are augmented by musicians from the Detroit Symphony Orchestra, who provide the strings, playing a fantastic arrangement written by Paul Riser, a trumpeter and arranger who would arrange some of Motown's biggest hits, including The Temptations' later hit 'Papa Was A Rolling Stone'.

However, when they added their vocals, The Temptations only had the bass, drums and guitar to record over, but once Robinson had added the strings and the 'sweetening' in the studio, Williams said the final mix was 'the most gorgeous, magical love song I'd ever heard. There was no question in our minds that we had the big one here.'

Conversely, in this memoir, Robinson claims that 'so many things were happening so quickly [at Motown] that I soon forgot about it', and only found out about the success of the song a few months later when Gordy told him. Although Robinson couldn't have known how successful the song would become, being perhaps his most successful composition, it's an interesting claim that he did not realise the song's greatness at the point of writing. That said, the rest of his autobiography is an equally brisk, breezy read, never dwelling on much for long.

The song was released on 21 December 1964, peaking on the charts three months later. It became the group's first US number one single on both the pop and R&B charts, yet thanks to Motown's lack of promotion in the UK, the song stalled at just number 43. Capitalising on this, Stax Records had Otis Redding record a version of the song just a few months later in July 1965 for his classic album, *Otis Blue*. His version is a more bluesy, horn-heavy affair that bears little resemblance to the more sophisticated orchestration of the original. Redding's rendition was a bigger hit in the UK than The Temptations' version, peaking at number 11. However, when The Temptations' version was reissued as a single in 1992, it peaked at an impressive number two in the UK, buoyed by its inclusion on the soundtrack to the film *My Girl*.

The group also recorded German and Italian versions of 'My Girl' ('Mein Girl' and 'Solamente Lei'), released in 1965 and 1966. They also sampled the song's introduction on their 1997 single 'Stay'. At Motown, both Stevie Wonder and a young Michael Jackson recorded their own versions of 'My Girl', serving as nothing more than album filler. Even Marvin Gaye released a version, although it wouldn't be released until after his death. The Temptations also recorded a hybrid version, mashed together with 'My Guy' to become 'My Guy, My Girl' with Diana Ross & The Supremes for their first album together.

'My Girl' gave The Temptations their first nomination for a Grammy in 1966 for 'Best Rhythm & Blues Recording', but they lost out to James Brown and his pioneering funk single, 'Papa's Got A Brand New Bag'.

'What Love Has Joined Together' (Smokey Robinson, Bobby Rogers)

Co-written by Robinson and fellow Miracle Bobby Rogers in 1962, Robinson first recorded the song with The Miracles before four other Motown acts got their chance to record it: Mary Wells, Barbara McNair (although her version wouldn't be unreleased until 2004), Syreeta and The Temptations.

Recorded here as a mid-tempo ballad, the vocals are suitably tight and sweet, with Kendricks delivering a fine, romantic lead. The backing vocals are equally sweet, if restrained, in keeping with the overall arrangement. Yet, as album filler goes, The Temptations' version is perfectly pleasant, featuring a string and horn arrangement that sits nicely behind Kendricks's lead vocal.

Robinson resisted the song on the album *What Love Has... Joined Together* in 1970. By this time, The Miracles had become Smokey Robinson & The Miracles, and on their version, Robinson delivers a sensual lead vocal backed by some equally smooth harmonies from the rest of The Miracles, with his wife Claudette prominent in the vocal mix. Their version, which is just shy of six minutes long, foreshadows Robinson's solo album *A Quiet Storm*, with its spacious, romantic arrangement.

'You'll Lose A Precious Love' (Smokey Robinson)
An early David Ruffin-led song, 'You'll Lose A Precious Love' is another Robinson-penned, typically sweet production, in which the narrator outlines to his partner what she'll lose if she leaves him. In typical Robinson fashion, the bright rhythm track, along with the Latin-style guitar strumming, masks this sad end to a relationship.

Interestingly, this isn't the gruff Ruffin that fans would become accustomed to. Here, he sings in a rather mellow way, rarely breaking his stride, while the rest of The Temptations back him with some equally smooth and relaxed vocals. There's no shouting or growling; instead, the result is a rather pedestrian performance from both Robinson in the arrangement and production, and some less-than-enthused vocals from Ruffin and the others. Franklin sings the last line of the bridge in a low rumble before handing the lead back to Ruffin to see the song to an unsatisfying end.

'It's Growing' (Smokey Robinson, Warren Pete Moore)
'It's Growing' was released as the follow-up single to 'My Girl' in March 1965, and given the success of its predecessor, Ruffin was given the lead. The song is classic Smokey Robinson, a tailor-made follow-up to capitalise on their new level of success, but sung with enough conviction from Ruffin to make it work. The lyrical content is reminiscent of 'The Way You Do The Things You Do', full of potentially laboured similes about love compared to various objects that expand or increase in size:

> Like a snowball rolling down the side of a hill,
> It's growing,
> Like the size of a fish that the man claims broke his reel,
> It's growing

Here, Robinson's protagonist has a love that is constantly increasing both in depth and intensity; it's a love that is inevitable and unstoppable. Not as captivating as 'My Girl' lyrically, the words are nonetheless cute and show Robinson's continued development as a songwriter. He was just 24 when he wrote both 'It's Growing' and 'My Girl', alongside his hits for The Miracles. It's no surprise, though, that the arrangement is also pretty close to 'My Girl', no doubt a deliberate choice, but this time Robinson threw all the resources Motown had at 'It's Growing'. It opens with a toy piano played by Earl Van Dyke of The Funk Brothers, before the rest of the band join in, complete with a lush orchestration, again featuring members from the Detroit Symphony Orchestra.

Above: Along with Smokey Robinson and Motown Founder Berry Gordy, The Temptations are pictured here in 1964, celebrating 'The Way You Do The Things You Do' becoming a smash national hit. (*Getty*)

Below: A 'Classic Five' publicity shot for Motown. (*James Kriegsmann*)

Above: A promotional picture of the 'Classic Five' lineup of Paul Williams, Eddie Kendricks, David Ruffin, Otis Williams and Melvin Franklin.

Left: The Temptations on *The Ed Sullivan Show* in 1969. (*Alamy*)

Unusually for The Temptations, who did all their background work themselves, Motown's in-house backing group, The Andantes, were added to the vocal mix in an attempt to achieve a bolder sound. This was standard practice at Motown, notably on the Four Tops singles written and produced by Holland-Dozier-Holland. They'd also fill in for the other Supremes on later singles. The backing vocals fit the familiar call-and-response pattern, but with the addition of The Andantes, it's hard to pick out the other Temptations.

While not as successful as 'My Girl', it was still a decent hit for the group, reaching number 18 on the pop charts and number three on the R&B chart. Interestingly, label-mates The Contours recorded a version featuring future Dennis Edwards on lead in 1967.

'Who's Lovin' You' (Smokey Robinson)
Originally recorded by The Miracles, appearing on their *Hi, We're The Miracles* album in 1961, Robinson clearly felt the song had enough potential to be re-recorded by The Temptations. At the very least, it guaranteed him extra publishing money. Ruffin sings the lead, and compared to his lead on 'My Girl', he sounds less sure of his talent; he's less the gruff, powerful Ruffin he would become. He grows into the song, but this is clearly a singer still finding his way in the group.

While this version doesn't necessarily add much to The Miracles' version, the background vocals are brighter, with Kendricks's soaring tenor sweetening the sound. Yet, the song here served as nothing more than album filler. Thankfully, it would be rescued from obscurity by a young Michael Jackson, whose version with his brothers on the Jackson 5's debut album became the definitive version, proving that Robinson's song was just waiting for the right voice.

'What's So Good About Goodbye' (Smokey Robinson)
Another early hit by The Miracles, their first version was a number-16 hit on the R&B chart and reached number 35 on the pop chart in 1961. The song was inspired by a television show Robinson saw, and, in Graham Betts' *Motown Encyclopaedia*, recalled:

> I was looking at the TV one night, and this woman and this man were talking. They were saying goodbye. They were lovers, you know, and she was asking him, 'What's good about that?' [The ending of a relationship] That was where it came from.

Robinson took this throwaway comment and turned it into one of the saddest songs he ever wrote, proving again his unique lyrical abilities: it goes beyond the typical break-up ballad (where usually the narrator is simply sad that the relationship is over) and instead questions the breakup process:

Well if leaving causes grieve
And depart can break your heart, tell me
What's so good about?
I could've done without it
What's so good about goodbye?

On the original, the instrumentation is led by Marv Tarplin, The Miracles' guitarist, before a surprisingly bold string arrangement comes in. The Temptations' version sounds much more polished and fresher than The Miracles' rendition, benefiting from Robinson's growing experience and confidence as a producer, as well the upgrade in technology at Hitsville's studios – Motown had originally started with basic two-track recording before upgrading in 1964 to a custom-built eight-track setup.

Kendricks sings the lead, again sounding not too dissimilar to Robinson himself, while the rest of The Temptations provide some suitably sweet backing vocals, although they are mixed fairly low compared with the rhythm track and horn arrangement in parts and, as a result, are hard to hear. Robinson corrects this in the outro, however, where they are much more audible.

'You Beat Me To The Punch' (Smokey Robinson, Ronald White)

First recorded by Mary Wells, her version was a top-ten pop hit in 1962 and would become her first R&B number one. Wells' version is breezy, almost calypso in its style, aided by male backing vocalists, the 'Love-Tones'. Later, when Wells needed backing, The Temptations themselves would sing behind her in some live performances. That, and it being another Robinson production, made sense for it to be included on *Sing Smokey*.

On this version, Paul Williams is given the lead, delivering a fine yet understated performance, retaining the power in his baritone. Given his deeper register, The Temptations' version doesn't quite match the breeziness of Wells' original; Williams' lead is more soulful, more aching, the opposite of what Robinson had Wells sing. The arrangement given to The Temptations is more straightforward, lacking any of the calypso influence of the original. It's not a bad cover, but it's equally clear this is nothing more than album filler.

'Way Over There' (Berry Gordy Jr, Smokey Robinson)

In the early days, Gordy developed a habit of releasing different versions of the same song if it gained traction in the marketplace in an attempt to boost sales. Several early singles, such as The Miracles' 'Shop Around', had different versions released, tweaked with new ideas. 'Way Over There' was one such song, also originally recorded by The Miracles, and two versions of the song were originally released by Motown: the first version appeared in February 1960 before Gordy had the group re-record it and released it two months later, this time with strings added to the mix, while the first version of the song gained some traction in regional marketplaces. In traditional Motown style, it would also be covered by others on the label, including Edwin Starr and the Marvelettes.

The Temptations' version retains their early doo-wop influences, with Franklin anchoring the harmonies with his trademark 'boom-booms' while the rest of the group harmonise on their repetition of 'come on, come on' in reply to Kendricks' lead vocal. Kendricks sounds particularly excellent here, aided by a swinging arrangement complete with funky horns. The versions by The Miracles are also doo-wop influenced: the first version sounds less well-rounded compared to the version with strings, but the vocals from Robinson and his bandmates are consistently excellent on both versions. The Temptations' version has a brighter, punchier feel which sounds more polished than the earlier versions by The Miracles.

'You've Really Got A Hold On Me' (Smokey Robinson)
Originally a hit for The Miracles, Robinson produces a very similar arrangement for The Temptations, including having both Kendricks and Paul Williams sing the opening in unison, as Robinson had with Bobby Rogers on their version. Kendricks sings the rest of the lead, again not dissimilar to Robinson's lead, making for a fairly run-of-the-mill cover. There's nothing new or exciting here, as this is merely a pleasant, if perhaps pointless, cover. Not even the most devoted Temptations fan would choose this over The Miracles' original version.

'(You Can) Depend On Me' (Berry Gordy Jr, Smokey Robinson)
Another early Miracles song, it was first released in September 1959 before a second version was released a year later, with Gordy re-recording the song in an attempt to increase sales. The first version is recorded pretty poorly: the instruments sound cluttered, and Robinson's lead vocal is so badly handled that it peaks as he hits the higher notes. Thankfully, the second version was better recorded: there's no distortion, and it sounds much warmer than its predecessor. Both are largely sparse affairs, with Marv Tarplin's guitar playing dominating the arrangement, and Robinson's silky-soft lead floating on top. That production today sounds dated, something of a throwback to the late 1950s, and (particularly the first version) is less polished or as finely mixed. Yet, the song is achingly beautiful, and foreshadowed the great Miracles ballads to come. Naturally, it would also be recorded by other Motown acts, including The Supremes, Mary Wells and the underrated Brenda Holloway.

Similar to their cover of 'You've Really Got A Hold On Me', this version is largely the same as that recorded by The Miracles, although the arrangement is bolder, featuring horns, giving it a more encompassing soundscape. Yet, the tempo remains similar and Kendricks sings the lead, no doubt as he was closer to Robinson's style of singing than the others. He delivers another excellent lead, with Otis Williams shadowing him in places, providing a contrasting vocal, as does Franklin when he vocalises in the later part of the song. Similar to 'Way Over There', this version is equally good as the original version, perhaps even slightly better, providing a decent finish to an overall strong second album from The Temptations.

The Temptin' Temptations (1965)

Personnel:
Otis Williams, Melvin Franklin, Paul Williams, Eddie Kendricks, David Ruffin: vocals
The Andates: backing vocals on 'Just Another Lonely Night'
Jimmy Ruffin: backing vocal on 'Born To Love You'
The Funk Brothers: instrumentation
Produced at Motown Hitsville USA, Detroit, by Smokey Robinson, Norman Whitfield, Ivy Jo Hunter, William 'Mickey' Stevenson between March 1964 and August 1965
Label: Gordy
Release date: 1 November 1965
Length: 31:33
Chart: US Pop: 11, US R&B: 1, UK: 40

Released just eight months after *Sing Smokey* hit the shelves, Motown was clearly looking to continue capitalising on the group's newfound success. A stronger album than *Meet The Temptations* and on a par with *Sing Smokey*, *The Temptin' Temptations* crammed 12 songs into just 31 minutes of music. Naturally, it follows a similar pattern to these two earlier albums: a combination of hit singles padded out with filler material, although the productions and songs themselves are better than some of the earlier material.

Here, though, there's more quality than pure filler: of the 12 songs included on *The Temptin' Temptations*, seven were released as singles, all charting on both the pop and R&B charts, an impressive feat. The album also brought together some newly written songs alongside singles that predated 'My Girl' but weren't included on *Sing Smokey*, including Smokey Robinson's 'I'll Be In Trouble' and Norman Whitfield's 'Girl (Why You Wanna Make Me Blue)', released in April and August 1964, respectively ('My Girl' was released in December 1964).

Despite the vocal talent in the group, *The Temptin' Temptations* features Ruffin on the bulk of the lead vocals. Kendricks still has his moments, but it was Paul Williams who was most negatively impacted by the success of Ruffin as the group's lead singer, with much less lead assigned to him. In his autobiography, Otis Williams recalled Paul Williams exclaiming, 'Shit, I can sing too!' When he was given the opportunity to sing lead, he would always produce an emotional, intense performance, yet few at Motown now had Paul in mind when writing for the group, being overlooked in favour of David Ruffin, particularly after the success of 'My Girl'. Here, he only sings two solo leads: 'Just Another Lonely Night' and one of his finest, Robinson's 'Don't Look Back'.

Producing duties, though, were somewhat more split: Robinson might have been the group's main producer, but others could still get their songs recorded by the group if they were good enough, and here, Norman Whitfield, William 'Mickey' Stevenson and Ivy Jo Hunter all get their turn. But it was Whitfield who was slowly beginning to chip away at Robinson's status as the group's main producer, and the tide would turn in his favour a year later with the release of the *Gettin' Ready* album.

Norman Whitfield had arrived at Motown as one determined and cocky man. He had long stalked The Temptations, getting close to their former manager Johnnie Mae Matthews (who looked after The Distants before they split), and eventually wound up at Motown via a stint at Thelma Records, run by Gordy's ex-wife, Thelma Coleman, and her mother, Hazel. When Gordy bought Thelma, Whitfield came with it and set about annoying almost anyone and everyone in his pursuit of recording his own compositions. However, determined as he was to become a writer and producer, he was also smart enough to absorb what was happening at Motown for his own benefit. Indeed, his contributions to *The Temptin' Temptations* are remarkably similar to Robinson's own style of writing and producing. If that's what it took to get one of his songs recorded by The Temptations, Whitfield would do it.

The album was another huge success for the group, topping the R&B albums charts and peaking at number 11 on the pop chart. Indeed, this success came very quickly after *Sing Smokey* dropped off the charts. The pace of releases, two albums per year, both charting with multiple hit singles, is almost unheard of today. But for The Temptations, it helped solidify their position at Motown as the company's prime male group.

'Since I Lost My Baby' (Smokey Robinson, Pete Moore)
The Temptin' Temptations opens with one of David Ruffin's best performances with the group, delivering an emotional, gut-wrenching lead vocal on one of Robinson's best songs. 'Since I Lost My Baby' is another breakup song, telling the story of a man whose world is no longer the same since his woman left him. Robinson and Moore's clever lyrics contrast the narrator's feelings with the positive portrayal of the world around him:

> Sun a-shining, there's plenty of life
> A new day is dawning sunny and bright
> But after I've been crying all night the sun is cold
> And the new day seems old

This approach continues into the second verse, where there are children playing happily in the streets and there's plenty of well-paid work available, 'but fun is a bore and with money I'm poor'.

In the first verse, Ruffin sings the lead while Franklin can be heard replying to Ruffin's first two lines, saying 'oh yeah' in his trademark rumble, helping to compound the misery of Ruffin's character. Ruffin's vocal builds in intensity as the song progresses, particularly on the line 'won't you *please* help me find her', the pleading emphasis on the 'please' highlighting the narrator's desperation. Like his recording on 'My Girl', Ruffin's voice is both gritty yet sweet, powerful yet vulnerable, reflecting the personality of Ruffin himself. Ruffin's upbringing had been difficult: his mother had died when he was just ten months old due to complications with his birth, and his father was frequently abusive towards him. As a result, he craved validation while at the same time being vulnerable and insecure, even if he projected confidence and charisma when in the spotlight. Behind that front lay a tormented soul

Meanwhile, the rest of the group provide some excellent backing vocals, replying to Ruffin's lines with more 'oh yeah's, as well as singing the track's title in the chorus. In his memoir, Otis Williams described 'Since I Lost My Baby' as 'one of my favourite songs', and in the notes to their *Gold* greatest hits collection, he later recalled:

> David enunciated so well. That was from Smokey; he showed him how to fit into that little pocket. And Eddie, that sweet tenor. He was calling out from the back. When Luther Vandross covered the song, I reflected that people were really listening.

Vandross, a devotee of classic soul, would cover the song for his second album *Forever, For Always, For Love* in 1982, taking a much softer, though no less emotional, approach to the song than Ruffin.

The Temptations' version was released as a single in the US in June 1965, the follow-up to 'It's Growing'. It reached almost the same position on both the R&B and pop charts, hitting number four and number 17, respectively.

'The Girl's Alright With Me' (Norman Whitfield, Eddie Holland, Eddie Kendricks)

A collaborative effort between Norman Whitfield, Eddie Holland and Eddie Kendricks, 'The Girl's Alright With Me' is a clear example of Whitfield's ability to absorb and learn from others at Motown, producing a song here with a similar style and theme to those Robinson had produced for the group.

The song tells the story of the narrator's partner, who is so incredibly attractive that she has multiple offers from other suitors on a daily basis but remains loyal to the narrator. Kendricks sings the lead, playing the part of a lovestruck narrator well, although Whitfield doesn't quite capture the beauty of his voice in the same way that Robinson was able to on 'The Way You Do The Things You Do'. His lead has a plainer quality, perhaps a deliberate choice, emphasising just how loyal the girl in the song is, even to this average everyman. Yet, Whitfield's strength lay in producing the instrumentation, which here is swinging, and the horn arrangement is big and brassy, creating a big-band-meets-soul feel. The other Temptations provide subtle backing in the verses, largely 'ooh's and 'ahh's, which become more prominent in the choruses.

Despite its strength, it was released as the B-side to the Robinson production 'I'll Be In Trouble', although this is arguably a better song. However, it did chart on its own accord as well, hitting number 39 on the US *Cashbox* R&B singles chart, but could only make number 102 on *Billboard*'s 'Bubbling Under the Hot 100' pop chart.

Following the standard Motown operating procedure of having their acts cover other Motown acts' songs, Whitfield would repeatedly record his compositions for different artists, and eventually, in 1974, he produced a new version of 'The Girl's Alright With Me' for the Undisputed Truth, one of his pet projects.

'Just Another Lonely Night' (Ivy Jo Hunter, William 'Mickey' Stevenson)
Perhaps the saddest song on *The Temptin' Temptations*, writers and producers Hunter and Stevenson crafted a song about a man lonely after the loss of his woman, perfect for the yearning baritone of Paul Williams. Like Whitfield, Stevenson and Hunter write in a style similar to Robinson lyrically, particularly the line 'That even in a crowd, laughing out loud, I'm lonely', reminiscent of Robinson's own signature song 'The Tracks Of My Tears'.

With the arrival of Ruffin and the success of singles with him singing lead, Paul Williams had few chances to sing lead compared to the earlier days, but when called upon, Williams sounded like he had something to prove, none more so than on 'Just Another Lonely Night'. He sounds like a man totally devastated by this heartbreak, like he's truly suffering. To contrast this deeply emotional performance, the backing vocals are much softer, bulked out by additional vocals from Motown's in-house female backing group The Andantes, like Robinson had on 'It's Growing'. This sweetness contrasts nicely with the despair of the lead vocal. It all adds up to be a forgotten gem in The Temptations' long discography.

Like countless other Motown songs, 'Just Another Lonely Night' was covered by others signed to the company; in this case, The Fantastic Four, Brenda Holloway and the Four Tops all recorded their own versions. Four Tops' version, however, wasn't released at the time and would only be rescued from the vaults in 2001 when it was included on their *Fourever* collection in 2001 – it features backing vocals from The Temptations themselves.

'My Baby' (Smokey Robinson, Pete Moore, Bobby Rodgers)
Essentially 'My Girl, Part 2', 'My Baby' is a much softer, breezy track, on which Ruffin sings about all the qualities his 'baby' has. Written by Robinson and his Miracles bandmates Moore and Rodgers, the lyrics are suitably Smokey sweet, helped by the bright and bouncy backing vocal arrangement the group devised. The backing vocals also mimic those on 'My Girl', as they repeat 'my baby, my baby, my baby' after the lead lines in the chorus.

Unsurprisingly, in trying to rewrite 'My Girl', the lyrics here aren't as strong, bordering on the exaggerated and silly in parts, and lines like 'Enough gold in her personality, to set Fort Knox to shame' haven't aged particularly well. Yet, this girl is so good that even Ruffin sings that if she doesn't like him as he is, 'if I have to change, you know I'm gonna do it for my baby'.

'My Baby' has a faster tempo than previous singles by the group, which were, up until this point, largely ballads, and although not a huge runaway success like 'My Girl', it still was a top-ten R&B hit and reached number 13 on the pop charts, even if the group have rarely performed it in the decades since.

'You've Got To Earn It' (Smokey Robinson, Cornelius Grant)
This is another Robinson-penned track, this time in collaboration with Cornelius Grant, a guitarist who became The Temptations' musical director and the unofficial 'Sixth Tempt'. He would tour with the group for several years – he can be heard playing guitar on all three of their live albums – and would contribute writing, playing on several Temptations hits. This was his first writing credit on a Temptations song.

It features another lead by Kendricks and a doo-wop influenced backing vocal arrangement from the rest of the group. Predictably, the song features more playful lyrics, by now Robinson's trademark, including lines such as:

> To get fire from a match, you've got to strike it (strike it, strike it, strike it)
> To get the feeling from a kiss, you've got to like it (like it, like, like it)

It's an innocent, uptempo number, perhaps not as strong as other Robinson-produced tracks, but it was deemed strong enough by Motown to include it on the B-side to 'Since I Lost My Baby', and it also charted, albeit at number 123 on *Billboard*'s 'Bubbling Under the Hot 100' chart. Still, not bad for an album track.

'Everybody Needs Love' (Norman Whitfield, Eddie Holland)
Another Whitfield-Holland collaboration, The Temptations were the first group to record it, although Whitfield would give it to a range of other Motown artists he produced in the years to come. Not released as a single, 'Everybody Needs Love' is nonetheless a decent album track, much better than other material recorded by the group to fill out these early albums. Again, Kendricks is given the lead, and gives another soft performance – in part matching the lyrics of the song, in which the narrator acknowledges the girl has been 'hurt before', promising that this time will be different. Yet, the girl simply doesn't want to rush into anything, and the narrator complains that he's willing to give her the love she wants, but she won't allow him.

The arrangement, much like 'The Girl's Alright With Me', is bold and brassy; there are even strings thrown into the mix. At times, this does sound a little cluttered, but it reflects the relative inexperience of Whitfield at this point in his career and his willingness to experiment. When the time came later, he'd learnt from past endeavours. Indeed, when he recorded the song again with Gladys Knight & The Pips, it was a top-ten hit on the R&B charts. Other Motown acts also recorded the song, filling the Jobete publishing coffers further, including Mary Wells, Jimmy Ruffin, Smokey Robinson & The Miracles and The Velvelettes. Whitfield somehow found the time to produce all these versions, even the version by The Miracles, with Robinson deferring to him on this occasion.

'Girl (Why You Wanna Make Me Blue)' (Norman Whitfield, Eddie Holland)

With 'Girl (Why You Wanna Make Me Blue)', Whitfield and Holland had cracked the Robinson writing code, producing a genuinely great song that sounded as if Motown's premier male star had written and produced it. Like Robinson's work with the group, the lyrics are direct and conversational – they ask the woman in question why she's so desperate to make the protagonist sad – while the mid-tempo groove and strong backbeat mask the hurt conveyed in the lyrics. It's sad, but it's also danceable.

Again, Whitfield gave the lead to Kendricks, who delivers a much better and fuller performance than 'Everybody Needs Love', his falsetto soaring particularly in the choruses as the other Temptations repeat the song's title. The arrangement is once again heavy on the horns from the start, while the Funk Brothers lay down a suitably funky groove, complete with loud handclaps throughout, giving it a party atmosphere.

Although it was included on *The Temptin' Temptations*, it was first released as a single in August 1964 before 'My Girl' was released, and because it was produced by Whitfield, it wasn't released on *Sing Smokey*. It was a hit single, too, hitting number 26 on the pop chart and number 11 on the R&B chart.

'Don't Look Back' (Smokey Robinson, Ronnie White)

The second lead from Paul Williams on *The Temptin' Temptations*, which became one of his signature songs. 'Don't Look Back' is one of Robinson's overlooked gems, a mournful, heart-achingly beautiful song that suits Williams' equally sorrowful voice perfectly. According to Otis Williams, Robinson wrote the song specifically for Paul because he had...

> ...[T]hat soulful, hurt sound. They sat together on the piano bench to work it out. The backgrounds were all Eddie's ideas. He was very creative in that way.

The song benefits from better lyrics from Robinson and White compared to other tracks on *The Temptin' Temptations*, and an almost jaunty arrangement, which combines both horns and strings, is both uplifting and sorrowful at the same time. But it's Williams' lead that makes the track: sure, Ruffin or maybe Kendricks could have done a decent job with 'Don't Look Back', but it perfectly fits Williams' soulful mournfulness. He doesn't try to oversing the lyrics, and he certainly doesn't try to emulate the gruffness or power of Ruffin; rather, his delivery is far more restrained, using his warm, melancholic baritone to give the song a tender feel. The song's often mournful feel somewhat disguises the lyrics, which aim to reassure the girl in the story that heartbreak and pain are often the price to pay for falling in love. However, once true love is found, there's no need to look back.

With hindsight of Williams' illness and tragic death, 'Don't Look Back' has taken on a sombre feel. In concert, the song became a central moment in the group's show, but after he left them in 1971, The Temptations never performed it again until they were inducted into the Rock & Roll Hall of Fame, where, along with Daryl Hall & John Oates, they sang the song in Paul's memory.

Despite the song's quality, it was only released as the B-side to 'My Baby', featuring Ruffin on the lead vocal. Nevertheless, the song did chart anyway, peaking at an impressive number 14 on the R&B chart, but only reaching number 83 on the pop chart. However, there can be no doubting that 'Don't Look Back' is the far superior song, one of the group's greatest ever recordings. An excellent version also appeared on their *Temptations Live!* album, which closed the original LP, with the women in the audience singing the chorus back at Williams, complete with plenty of screams and applause.

'I Gotta Know How' (Norman Whitfield, Eddie Holland)
After the melancholy of 'Don't Look Back', *The Temptin' Temptations* returns to the more familiar territory of uptempo love songs, once again with Kendricks on lead. Given that Whitfield's big break with the group would come with him having Ruffin sing the lead on 'Ain't Too Proud To Beg', it's interesting that, on his early recordings with the group, he gave most of the lead to Kendricks. This track sounds like album filler and could easily be a rework of 'Girl (Why You Wanna Make Me Blue)' in parts, particularly when the horns kick in. It's a pleasant album track, but one of the more forgettable moments on this collection.

'Born To Love You' (Ivy Jo Hunter, William 'Mickey' Stevenson)
The second Hunter-Stevenson production on the album, 'Born To Love You' is a stronger album cut than 'I Gotta Know How', even if its doo-wop influence sounds more like the tracks on *Meet The Temptations* or *Sing Smokey,* particularly Franklin's bass vocals, which appear throughout. Kendricks sings the lead once more, although interestingly, Ruffin sings the bridge, foreshadowing the sharing of leads in a single song later in the group's career, which Whitfield would utilise on their upcoming single 'You're My Everything'.

Lyrically, the song is less innocent than some of the Robinson tracks on the album, with the narrator telling his girl that he'd rather die than be without her. The group would revisit this darker approach to ballads on their *Wish It Would Rain* album.

'I'll Be In Trouble' (Smokey Robinson)
First released as a single in April 1964, for some reason, it was not included on *Sing Smokey* earlier in 1965. Perhaps Motown were simply trying to save decent material for another Temptations album. As a result, listening to *The Temptin' Temptations* in full, this track sounds slightly more dated than the more recently recorded tracks, a throwback to the earlier, less-established 'Motown Sound'. Yet, it's nonetheless an early gem from the group, with another lead by Kendricks and Franklin providing the doo-wop influence with his bass vocals.

Sonically, 'I'll Be In Trouble' clearly tries to replicate 'The Way You Do The Things You Do', although somewhat less successfully. Motown, at least in the earlier years, would often exploit a concept or sound as much as possible to create a similar-sounding hit. The story also treads the same ground: the narrator is so in love with his girl that 'no matter what you do or say, I know I'm gonna love you anyway', and if she leaves, he'll be in trouble. It's a simple, teenage love story, but The Temptations carry it off with enough conviction for it not to sound terribly old-fashioned.

Released as a single, it was a moderate hit for the group, reaching number 33 on the pop chart and number 22 on the R&B chart, but not enough of a success for Robinson. This meant that Whitfield could have the next A-side single release for The Temptations, with 'Girl (Why You Wanna Make Me Blue)' issued as the follow-up single.

'You're The One I Need' (Smokey Robinson)
The final track on *The Temptin' Temptations* is yet another lead from Kendricks, with additional vocals from Ruffin and Paul Williams in the bridge. The song is more album filler, certainly not strong enough for a single release, but it has a breezy, pop feel, complete with a raging saxophone solo that keeps it anchored in R&B.

The song is, predictably, about another love that the narrator simply cannot do without. In the first verse Kendricks sings, 'Love somebody sweet/Love somebody kind/Love somebody who won't/Leave you behind'. However, in the chorus, Robinson writes that these things don't matter in reality, 'Cause when you love somebody, no matter who/Then that's the one you need'. Perhaps not the most romantic lyric Robinson ever wrote, a backhanded compliment at best, it's nonetheless a perfectly pleasant, if largely forgettable, end to *The Temptin' Temptations*.

Gettin' Ready (1966)

Personnel:
Otis Williams, Melvin Franklin, Paul Williams, Eddie Kendricks, David Ruffin: vocals
The Funk Brothers: instrumentation
Produced at Hitsville USA, Detroit, by Smokey Robinson, Norman Whitfield, Robert Staunton, Robert Walker, William 'Mickey' Stevenson, Sylvester Potts, Marv Johnson between October 1963 and January 1963
Label: Gordy
Release date: 15 June 1966
Length: 31:33
Chart: US pop: 12, US R&B: 1, UK: 40

Released some seven months after *The Temptin' Temptations*, *Gettin' Ready* sought to capitalise on the group's latest singles: the Smokey Robinson song 'Get Ready' and Norman Whitfield's 'Ain't Too Proud To Beg'. The release of these two singles marked a new chapter for the group, with the success of Whitfield's production effectively ending Robinson's hold over the group, replacing him as the group's primary producer on most of their subsequent single and album releases.

This happened largely as a result of the relatively modest success of the single 'Get Ready', released in early 1966. Company policy at Motown dictated that the producer who last had a hit with an artist would have the next single release on them, too, subject to approval at the company's Friday morning quality control meeting. Whitfield, though, was impatient and wanted to release his song, 'Ain't Too Proud To Beg', as the next Temptations single. Yet, Gordy would not budge: Smokey Robinson had the biggest hits with the group so far, so 'Get Ready' would be next.

He did, however, make a concession to Whitfield: if 'Get Ready' failed to break the top ten on the pop charts, he would release 'Ain't Too Proud To Beg'. Despite the promotional activities of the company and the group, the song stalled, reaching just number 29 on the pop charts (although it took the top spot on the R&B chart). Gordy kept his word to Whitfield, and, in May 1966, released 'Ain't Too Proud To Beg', which also topped the R&B charts and peaked at number 13 on the pop chart. As Gordy recalled in his memoir, 'Get Ready' was a 'crack in Smokey's armour. That was all Norman Whitfield needed.'

As a result, both singles appear on *Gettin' Ready*, as do other productions from both Robinson and Whitfield, but other Motown producers got the chance to record the group, albeit for album tracks rather than singles, such as William 'Mickey' Stevenson and Ivy Jo Hunter. *Gettin' Ready*, though, marks the end of any serious future involvement from Robinson in terms of writing and producing The Temptations. A few of his songs recorded on the group would appear on their next album *With A Lot O' Soul*, though none would be single releases; he contributed a song on their *Wish It Would Rain* album, and later produced a couple of so-so tunes for their *Reunion* album in 1982, and eventually produced and duetted with the group on 'Is It Gonna Be Yes Or No' on their 2022 album *Temptations 60*.

The album artwork, reflecting the title, features a photograph of the group getting ready for a performance in a shared dressing room, donning their tight-fitting three-piece suits, doing their hair, and Ruffin adjusting his glasses. There's no sign of the bickering and division that was beginning to flare up among the five members, with each posing individually, fully fitted out in their stage-wear, for the back cover.

Yet, *Gettin' Ready* did mark a turning point with respect to The Temptations' relationship with each other. With the success of 'Ain't Too Proud To Beg', all future singles would feature Ruffin on lead, with the exception of 'You're My Everything', on which he shared the lead with Kendricks. Naturally, this fed into Ruffin's ego: he saw himself as the focal point of the group, and began distancing himself from the other members, travelling alone to shows in his own monogrammed car. The others were uneasy with such shows of wealth and arrogance, but no-one could deny Ruffin's talent or success.

'Say You' (Charles Jones, Robert Dobyne, Robert Staunton)

Gettin' Ready opens with 'Say You', a beautiful ballad led by David Ruffin, which has him playing the part of an insecure lover who begs his lover to affirm her love for him. It's a different role for Ruffin than usual; normally, either he's done wrong and begs for forgiveness or he's trying to woo yet another woman. Here, though, playing the part of this vulnerable, almost needy, man, he sings in a much more restrained manner than his usual powerful, gruff preaching style of singing.

Produced by Robert Staunton and Robert Walker, they deftly combine the Motown beat with a gorgeous string arrangement, allowing the vocals of Ruffin and the other Temptations to sit comfortably on top. Franklin contributes a line in the bridge before handing back to Ruffin, who ramps up the ante as the song comes to a close, but his performance isn't as powerful as others on *Gettin' Ready*.

Recorded first by The Temptations in June 1965, in a quirk of fate, the song was covered by The Monitors a month later and released as a single in November 1965 featuring Richard Street, a former member of The Distants and future Temptation, on lead vocals. It was a minor R&B hit for The Monitors and was included on their only Motown album release, *Greetings! We're The Monitors*, in 1968.

'Little Miss Sweetness' (Smokey Robinson)

Another sweet song from Robinson, 'Little Miss Sweetness' tells the story of all the 'sweet things' the narrator loves about his girl. It's essentially a reworking of 'The Way You Do The Things You Do', Ruffin singing in a vocal style that is more gruff than sweet and is certainly more gritty than on 'Say You', especially in the choruses. The backing vocals are limited largely to 'ooh's and repeating the song's title in the choruses.

Lyrically, it follows earlier Robinson songs, with plenty of metaphors and incredibly saccharine lyrics. For example, verse two goes:

If ever a man had a sweet tooth, I have one indeed
I order cookies and cakes, and malts and shakes
From the menus that I read
But all the cakes and shakes and malts I've bought put together don't exceed
The sweetness in just one of your kisses
Baby, you're the one I need

It's teenage fluff, which sounds a little dated today, but at the time, no doubt, was good enough for at least a release on an album as filler, if not as a single. Always keen to re-record such songs on other acts as album filler, Motown also released a version by The Isley Brothers on their 1967 album *Soul On The Rocks*.

'Ain't Too Proud To Beg' (Edward Holland Jr, Norman Whitfield)
With only modest success with The Temptations so far, Whitfield knew he had a potential hit with 'Ain't Too Proud To Beg', a fiery R&B groove that was far grittier and punchier than almost anything the group had recorded so far, especially compared to the pop-soul of Robinson's 'Get Ready'; Otis Williams would describe the difference between the two songs as 'night and day'. Written in collaboration with Eddie Holland, who provided the lyrics, Whitfield pressured Berry Gordy to release it as the group's next single. Whitfield, though, had to present it to Motown's 'quality control' meetings, held every Friday, where producers and department heads would discuss the quality of material presented and vote on single releases. Given that The Temptations were one of the label's most popular groups, they could be especially harsh on anything recorded on them, sending it back to the producer in question to be worked on some more. As Berry Gordy recalled in his autobiography:

> At the Friday meeting, Norman sat confidently as we listened to his new production on the Tempts – 'Ain't Too Proud To Beg'. The reactions were mixed, from 'I hate it' to 'It's a big hit'. I was the last one to give my opinion. 'I love the feel – it's street', I said. 'But it doesn't have enough meat. I gotta hear more story.'
>
> The next week, Norman was back with an improved 'Ain't Too Proud To Beg'. It got more votes, but was again rejected. Norman looked crushed when the group went along with my 'Not quite there.' But the following week, he was back – and taking no prisoners. David Ruffin's voice came jumping off that record, begging like I'd never heard before.

Given the song's lyrics – a guy desperately pleading for his girl not to leave him – and the song's funky instrumentation, Whitfield gave Ruffin the lead. From the opening line, Ruffin plays the character to perfection, pleading desperately for his woman to take him back, as he growls, 'I *know* you wanna leave me, but I refuse to let you go'. The vocal is much less restrained than previous Ruffin-led songs, showcasing his powerful macho side but also his softer, vulnerable side. After all, he really wants this girl back.

The key to Ruffin's performance was Whitfield forcing him to sing in a higher key than usual. Williams recalled watching Ruffin recording his lead vocals, sweat pouring off his face, his trademark glasses falling off his face, while Whitfield simultaneously encouraged and demanded more. This might have punished his vocal cords, but it resulted in a more raw, gruffer lead vocal than anything Robinson had gotten out of Ruffin, reflecting the song itself. Whitfield might have started his work with The Temptations recording Robinson-a-likes, but now he was beginning to forge his own musical direction. Some elements remained the same, including the tight backing vocals and the saxophone solo, which was a feature of their earlier recordings, too, but this certainly had a grittier edge.

Whitfield's faith in the song was justified: when it was finally released as a single in May 1966, it became a number-one R&B hit and peaked at number 13 on the pop chart, a marked improvement on 'Get Ready'. The group included it on the live albums, featuring on *Temptations Live!*, *Live At The Copa* and the soundtrack to the NBC television special with The Supremes, *TCB*.

'Get Ready' (Smokey Robinson)

Today considered one of the group's greatest songs, it was not a pop hit on the same level as 'My Girl'. Smooth yet danceable, it 'lacked an edge', according to Otis Williams, who recalled that it 'wasn't cute or sweet, and it wasn't a ballad. Smokey has called it the most direct song he ever wrote.'

The lyrics are typically Robinson-esque, although there's less emphasis on the metaphors; rather, the song's narrator is very direct in his seduction method:

> I never met a girl who makes me feel the way that you do
> (You're alright)
> Whenever I'm asked who makes my dreams real
> I say that you do
> (You're outta sight)
> So fee fi fo fum
> Look out baby 'cause here I come

It is certainly more direct than 'My Girl' or 'My Baby', but the sentiment is the same. Kendricks takes the lead with Franklin doubling the vocal on the 'fee fi fo fum' line, and all the others on the 'You're all right' responses. The Funk Brothers lay down an infectious, fast-paced groove: the drumming is intense, and the song is filled out by James Jamerson's bass playing, which is mixed high, along with a punchy horn arrangement. The horns are particularly loud in the introduction, and were re-worked for their live shows so that on each horn stab, a different member would take up a position with their arms raised in a 'V' shape before Kendricks started the lead vocal and the others began their synchronised dance routine. Paul Williams devised the choreography in a hotel room before an appearance on the American Bandstand television show, and The Temptations continue to perform a version of the routine today. Kendricks, as the lead, provides a softer counterpoint to all this, his falsetto rising above and gliding over the arrangement. He sounds confident and breezes through the vocal with ease. If that wasn't enough, there are also strings, though they are mostly overwhelmed by the horns and rhythm.

It was the last song released as a single to feature Kendricks as the sole lead singer until 'Please Return Your Love To Me', from the *Wish It Would Rain* album. Indeed, with the success of 'Ain't Too Proud To Beg', Ruffin came to dominate the releases.

The lack of chart success didn't deter Motown from having its other acts record the song, though. 'Get Ready' found new life with several acts, including The Supremes in 1966, Rare Earth in 1970 and even Smokey Robinson & The Miracles in 1970. Robinson recorded the song twice more: a disco version appeared on his *Where There's Smoke…* album in 1979, and he included the song on his album *Smokey & Friends* in 2014 as a duet with Take That's Gary Barlow. Perhaps the best cover, though, is Ella Fitzgerald's, released in 1969, produced by Richard Perry, who, decades later, produced The Temptations' album *For Lovers Only*, released in 1995.

'Lonely, Lonely Man Am I' (Eddie Holland, Eddie Kendricks, Norman Whitfield)

Another collaboration between Whitfield, Holland and Kendricks, 'Lonely, Lonely Man Am I' stands in contrast to 'Get Ready' thanks to its depressing nature. The song opens with Franklin singing the line 'lonely, I'm so lonely' mournfully; Franklin, normally a beacon of positivity and described by Williams as the 'heart' of The Temptations, sounds uncharacteristically sad here.

Whitfield gives the lead to Paul Williams, a sensible choice given the sorrowful depths of his baritone, and he delivers a gut-wrenching performance. His pleading is all the more poignant today, given his later publicised personal struggles and suicide. Williams plays the part of a lonely man convincingly, perhaps drawing on his own experience of being slowly isolated in the group, at least when it came to dishing out the lead vocals.

In typical Motown fashion, the song was later recorded by Jimmy Ruffin, Chuck Jackson (when he was briefly signed to the label) and The Velvelettes, who retitled the song 'Lonely, Lonely Girl Am I'.

'Too Busy Thinking About My Baby' (Janie Bradford, Barrett Strong, Norman Whitfield)

Better known as a hit for Marvin Gaye, The Temptations recorded an earlier version, with Kendricks on lead. However, it was first recorded by Jimmy Ruffin in 1964, with different lyrics and titled 'I Know How To Love Her', but was shelved and remained unreleased until 2002. Yet, Whitfield knew the song still had potential and, along with his co-writers, came up with new lyrics and recorded it with The Temptations a year later.

The song was written in collaboration with Janie Bradford, an early key Motown employee who had previously co-written Motown's first major hit, 'Money (That's What I Want)', which was recorded by none other than Barrett Strong. Strong's singing career, though, had failed to take off, and he instead turned his attention to songwriting. Indeed, this song marks the first of his writing contributions for The Temptations with Whitfield, a partnership that would last for the next five years, with Strong usually writing the lyrics to Whitfield's ever more experimental arrangements.

Lyrically, Bradford, Strong and Whitfield had clearly taken lessons at the Smokey Robinson school of balladry, as the song tells the story of a man who simply cannot think about anything else other than his baby. He can't read the newspaper, watch TV, or even consider his future; his 'one-track' mind doesn't give him the time for anything else. It's a world away from the dark message songs that Whitfield and Strong would soon be writing for the group.

However, unlike the more familiar Gaye version, in which he sang in a much more powerful way than he was comfortable with, Kendricks sings softly and sweetly, backed by The Funk Brothers' relaxed and swinging arrangement.

While not released as a single for The Temptations, Motown released it as the follow-up single to Gaye's mega-hit 'I Heard It Through The Grapevine' in 1969, reaching number one on the R&B singles chart and going to number four on the pop charts (and number five on the UK Singles Chart). It was Gaye's second-biggest hit of the 1960s, but his performance owes a lot to Ruffin's style of singing. When producing Gaye, Whitfield would force him to sing in a higher-than-comfortable key, giving the resulting vocal an intense pleading quality. Whitfield did this, of course, on 'Ain't Too Proud To Beg' with Ruffin. Whitfield later recalled in an interview with Paul Zollo that it was one of his favourite compositions.

A version was also recorded by Jimmy Ruffin with the new lyrics, but that, too, wouldn't be released until decades later. Similarly, The Monitors also recorded a decent version, released on their retrospective album *Say You! The Motown Anthology 1963 – 1968*.

'I've Been Good To You' (Smokey Robinson)

This was first recorded by The Miracles in 1961 and initially released as a B-side to their hit 'What's So Good About Goodbye'. The song is a mournful ballad, telling the story of a man who has been nothing but good to his girl, yet inexplicably she's decided to leave. Unsurprisingly, the song's narrator doesn't take this well, telling her she'll be back crying for forgiveness. Given the song's depressing feel, it's an odd choice for Kendricks to sing lead on; he certainly does a fine job, but it might have suited Paul Williams better, given that sorrowful ballads were his forte. The production is fairly muted compared with the rest of *Gettin' Ready*, especially the horn section, which is mixed low along with the backing vocals in the verses.

It was released later as the B-side to 'You're My Everything' in 1967, and fellow Motown artist Brenda Holloway also recorded a version. Her version is probably the best of all them all; her commanding performance gives the song greater emotional weight, conveying a sense of vulnerability not found in the others.

'It's A Lonely World Without Your Love' (Ivy Jo Hunter, William 'Mickey' Stevenson)

In classic Motown style, the uptempo danceable beat and bright horn arrangement mask the sadness of Hunter's and Stevenson's lyrics. Kendricks is given the lead and the rest of the group provide some excellent call-and-response backing vocals throughout, as well as repeating 'lonely, lonely world without you' throughout the final verse. The song swings thanks to both the Funk Brothers laying down a tight, Motown groove – the drums are locked in tightly with the bass, over which handclaps are layered and horns blare their way through a bold arrangement. It's perhaps more reminiscent of Four Tops' classics than previous Temptations hits, but it's one of the more enjoyable filler tracks on *Gettin' Ready*.

'Fading Away' (Pete Moore, Smokey Robinson, Bobby Rodgers)

Along with his Miracles colleagues Pete Moore and Bobby Rodgers, Robinson wrote and produced a real lost gem with 'Fading Away', a beautifully sad song featuring some gorgeous lead vocals from Kendricks. On this song, the breakup theme is tweaked as there's no declaration of heartbreak or pain; rather, Kendricks, as the narrator, is more introspective, focusing on the slow demise of his relationship. Kendricks' character knows his relationship is 'fading away' as his girl 'has changed, and it's showing' – she's no longer in love with him. The lyrics are similar to Robinson's previous efforts with the group, heavy on the metaphors in the first verse, particularly:

> The feeling we used to get whenever our lips met
> Like smoke from a cigarette, it's fading away
> Fading away, fading away
> It hurts me to think about how love where there was no doubt
> Like a cloud when the sun comes out, it's fading away
> Fading away, fading away

The string arrangement is equally gorgeous, conveying a sense of tension and foreboding, making the point that the relationship is reaching its inevitable end.

It was released as the B-side to 'Get Ready', making it a double header for Kendricks on lead. Given the song's strength, it's somewhat surprising that it was only covered twice by other Motown artists, Bobby Taylor & The Vancouvers and The Velvelettes. Later, Daryl Hall and John Oates – both huge fans of The Temptations – covered it in 2004 on their *Our Kind Of Soul* album, but The Temptations' version has yet to be bettered.

'Who You Gonna Run To' (Smokey Robinson)

Another strong album cut, 'Who You Gonna Run To' is the second and final lead by Paul Williams on *Gettin' Ready* and, unsurprisingly, it's another sad ballad. The song is a variation on Robinson's approach to such songs: fed up with this girl running to him when things go wrong in her relationships, Williams' character has had enough. It's an unusually bitter song for Robinson, but it makes a change from his usual fare.

The song starts with a fairly loose, laid-back arrangement, just guitar, drums and bass, before a sweet string section is mixed in and the backing vocals join in for the chorus. As the song goes on, Williams becomes more exasperated in his lead, reflecting the frustration of the main character.

'You're Not An Ordinary Girl' (Pete Moore, Smokey Robinson, Marc Tarplin, Ronnie White)

Co-written with his partners in The Miracles, 'You're Not An Ordinary Girl' is another unusually direct track from Robinson. With Kendricks on lead yet again, he sings about the special qualities of his girl, who is sweet 'like candy'. The first verse makes it clear that the girl isn't a literal angel – 'you ain't got no halo hangin' over your head' – but that doesn't matter to Kendricks, as she's as close to divinity as possible. It's plenty sweet and perhaps a little corny listening back today, but it's not bad as mere album filler, with its direct nature making it essentially 'Get Ready' part two. Motown clearly felt it was strong enough for a B-side release at least, featuring on the flip side to the future Whitfield-produced single 'Beauty's Only Skin Deep'.

'Not Now (I'll Tell You Later)' (Smokey Robinson, Otis Williams)

A rare writing credit for Otis Williams during this period, it's perhaps most notable for featuring The Supremes on backing vocals – they are mixed surprisingly high in the final mix, especially after the two-minute mark.

Culled from an earlier session when Eldridge 'Al' Byrant was still in the group, it was presumably felt strong enough for inclusion on *Gettin' Ready* and meant no further costs would be incurred in recording something else (it also guaranteed some publishing for both Robinson and Williams). As a result, the overall sound is something of a throwback compared to 'Get

Ready' or 'Ain't Too Proud To Beg'. It's more doo-wop influenced and sounds more dated in comparison with the rest of the album.

Nevertheless, there is a certain charm to it, almost like a house party in which the group are joined by their friends, which, in this case, just happens to be The Supremes, at this point consisting of Diana Ross, Mary Wilson and Florence Ballard. Kendricks sings the lead, and towards the end, he vocalises with Ballad, their falsetto and soprano voices, respectively, intertwining. Being taken from an older session, it also has more of a doo-wop feel than their most recent work. There's also a saxophone solo halfway through, and handclaps. Not the strongest song the group would ever record, but a cute track, nonetheless.

Bonus Tracks On The 1999 CD Reissue

'Give It Up' (Sylvester Potts, Mary Wells)

Co-written by Motown's first female star, Mary Wells, and Sylvester Potts, a singer with The Contours, this was not originally released on *Gettin' Ready*, but was included as part of the 1999 CD reissue. It features Paul Williams on lead, who delivers a deeply emotional lead performance, which is contrasted by the light doo-wop backing vocals, which, at times, distract from the depth of Williams' performance. Like many of the early Motown tracks, it's heavy on the use of a baritone sax and has an unrelenting beat.

'The Man Who Doesn't Believe In Love' (Marv Johnson)

The final bonus song on the 1999 CD reissue was written by Marv Johnson, whose single 'Come To Me' would be the first to be issued by Tamla Records, the precursor to the Motown Record Corporation. Johnson had his own version of this song released in 1963, as the B-side to 'Unbreakable Love' on United Artists Records (Johnson recorded at Motown's Hitsville Studios, but most of his releases were distributed by United Artists, who then signed him to their label).

It begins with an almost marching drum beat before Paul Williams begins his lead vocal. The song tells the story of a man who shuns love, with Williams asking the questions: 'Does he know what he's been missing? The lovely girls he could been kissing?'

Presumably recorded before the album's singles, it also sounds more like a throwback, especially with the doo-wop style backing vocals, and had it been included on *Gettin' Ready* the first time around, it would have been simply more filler.

With A Lot O' Soul (1967)

Personnel:
Otis Williams, Melvin Franklin, Paul Williams, Eddie Kendricks, David Ruffin: vocals
The Andantes: backing vocals on 'All I Need'
Cornelius Grant: guitar
The Funk Brothers: instrumentation
Produced at Hitsville USA, Detroit, by Norman Whitfield, Smokey Robinson, Frank Wilson, Brian Holland, Lamont Dozier and Ivy Jo Hunter between March 1966 and February 1967
Label: Gordy
Release date: 17 July 1967
Length: 34:52
Chart: US pop: 7, US R&B: 1, UK: 19

Although the standard narrative has The Temptations at this point solely as a Norman Whitfield group, *With A Lot O' Soul* is actually much more of a collaborative effort than often portrayed. The often-told story that once 'Get Ready' flopped (or, at least, wasn't a sufficiently big hit) and was eclipsed by 'Ain't Too Proud To Beg' masks the fact that Whitfield, at least on this album, had not quite yet completely taken over. Whitfield did produce the bulk of the album, but older recordings by Smokey Robinson provided the 'filler' to bulk out the track list, while Frank Wilson produced 'All I Need', Ivy Jo Hunter produced 'Sorry Is A Sorry Word', and even Brian and Eddie Holland and Lamont Dozier were able to contribute, despite The Temptations not being typically considered an 'H-D-H' group.

Naturally, the album features the standard collection of hit singles – '(I Know) I'm Losing You', 'All I Need' and 'You're My Everything' – and the usual album filler. Yet, the singles hinted at a new, more modern direction for the group, with new guitar sounds in particular, aided by their musical director, Cornelius Grant, whose guitar riffs are sharper and more aggressive, bringing a greater funk element to the tracks. Similarly, the basslines are funkier and more pronounced and the horn stabs are much tighter, drawing influence from James Brown's approach to using horns as percussive instruments. As a result, *With A Lot O' Soul* achieves a grittier edge than earlier Temptations albums.

Overall, *With A Lot O' Soul* is one of the group's more consistent efforts from their 'Classic Five' period. Naturally, Ruffin and, to a lesser extent, Kendricks dominated the lead vocals on the album, although both Otis and Paul Williams were given one lead each on the album, with Paul in particular proving he could still deliver when, however rarely, called upon. Yet, even the album tracks on here, the filler, are much stronger than on previous Temptations albums.

Though, as Otis Williams wrote in his autobiography, by this point:

> The concept of The Temptations as a group with several lead singers basically ended, at least as far as the records went, and David dominated the

> singles until he left the group. This wasn't intentional; it's just how it happened. We all felt that more songs should have been cut [recorded] on Paul, and he still complained. When it came to creative decisions, folks at Motown might hear you out, but that's as far as it went.

Indeed, Motown had little incentive to give more leads to Temptations not named Ruffin, given the success of the singles with him on lead vocals. Paul Williams' 'Don't Look Back' might now be considered one of the group's greatest hits, but it was a relatively modest hit compared to the likes of 'My Girl', so he had to make do with album cuts or nothing at all. He would also begin drinking more heavily around this time – he never drank when the group started out – and he was also having personal problems and financial worries. Kendricks, too, suffered, sharing lead vocals on 'You're My Everything', but not getting a single release with him on lead.

Added to this was David Ruffin's ever-growing ego; by this point, Ruffin had begun to feel like it was his group, and he should be compensated appropriately, as well as having the group billed appropriately, like Diana Ross & The Supremes or Smokey Robinson & The Miracles. This, of course, was a non-starter, and the others didn't agree with Ruffin. No-one at this point wanted to see Ruffin leave the group – could they survive such a loss? – but even then, they kept their eyes and ears open for a potential replacement. Around this time, Otis Williams and Kendricks first came across Dennis Edwards performing with fellow Motown act The Contours, and they kept him in mind as things began to deteriorate.

The group's issues with Ruffin wouldn't come to a head yet, though, and *With A Lot O' Soul* was another hit album for the group, hitting the top spot on the R&B charts, reaching number seven on the pop chart and even reaching number 19 on the UK albums charts.

'(I Know) I'm Losing You' (Cornelius Grant, Eddie Holland, Norman Whitfield)

Released as a single in November 1966, '(I Know) I'm Losing You' is a funk workout that James Brown would have been proud to record. It's a gritty slice of R&B that first emerged from Cornelius Grant, a guitarist with The Temptations' road band who would become their musical director. Grant came up with the opening riff, which Whitfield overheard one day during a jam session. Along with Eddie Holland, the trio crafted the rest of the song, finally recording the single in September 1966.

The song opens with Grant playing his guitar riff, which is both bluesy and funky at the same time, before the rest of the Funk Brothers, and Ruffin on lead vocals, fall in. The bass thunders along with growing intensity, giving the track a sense of foreboding as the narrator slowly loses his love – perfect, once again, for the womanising David Ruffin. His vocal is intense, matched by an equally powerful horn arrangement written by Paul Riser, while the rest of

The Temptations counterpoint with more sweet 'oooh's and repetitions of the 'I'm losing you' line. The horns take the intensity up a notch further around the two-minute mark before the focus returns to Ruffin, who also intensifies his already powerful lead.

It became another number-one R&B single for The Temptations, and peaked at number eight on the US pop charts, as well as reaching number 19 on the UK singles chart. Yet, in true Whitfield fashion, having a hit with The Temptations with '(I Know) I'm Losing You' wasn't enough, and he later recorded an experimental ten-minute version with Rare Earth, a rock-funk band that Whitfield took under his wing. Their version was also a hit, reaching number eight on the US pop charts.

'Ain't No Sun Since You've Been Gone' (Cornelius Grant, Sylvia Moy, Norman Whitfield)

Another Grant-Whitfield track, this time in collaboration with Sylvia Moy, whose main duties revolved around looking after a young Stevie Wonder, this song once again uses the imagery of the sun and darkness in another relationship gone sour. It also uses the Motown tried-and-tested method of disguising the sadness of the lyrics with a pounding beat and danceable track. If anything, the song's title foreshadowed Bill Withers' hit 'Ain't No Sunshine', in which he, too, sings of a lack of sunshine once his girl has left.

Produced by Whitfield, Ruffin sounds unleashed, his moans, groans and growls all powerful, all soulful. The backing vocals are mostly absent until the bridge, when the rest of The Temptations can be properly heard, with the instrumentation broken down to largely just bass and percussion.

A few months later, in September 1967, Gladys Knight & The Pips released their own version, as did Chuck Jackson a year later. Predictably, both The Undisputed Truth and Rare Earth also recorded their own versions, in 1971 and 1976, respectively. Diana Ross & The Supremes also recorded a version, but it was not released until 2008 on *Let The Music Play: Supreme Rarities – 1960-1969 – Motown Lost & Found.*

'All I Need' (Frank Wilson, Eddie Holland, R. Dean Taylor)

Norman Whitfield might have been on his way to dominate recordings by The Temptations, but other Motown producers could still get their material recorded by the group if it was deemed strong enough, especially if you happened to be one of his protégées like Frank Wilson. Wilson had initially attempted a solo career at Motown before Berry Gordy redirected his creative energies to writing and producing (his single 'Do I Love You (Indeed I Do)' was shelved from release, but a demo found its way to the UK and the Northern Soul scene, becoming a classic).

'All I Need' is such a song: a brilliant piece of danceable heartbreak, featuring that classic, pounding Motown beat that masks the yearning, pleading lyrics in which Ruffin begs his woman to forgive his infidelity with another. Otis Williams reflected later that it was no surprise that many of their big hits featured similar stories of heartbreak and cheating: for Williams, this was what their female audience wanted to hear, their guys 'pleading, begging, confessing and basically admitting their mistakes.' Ruffin is at his most powerful on 'All I Need'; it's a gut-wrenching, electrifying lead vocal that ranks with his best.

The arrangement is simultaneously light and heavy. The rhythm section groove along, almost jauntily, but this is contrasted by the heavy horn arrangement and the baritone saxophone that plays throughout the track – a technique Motown had perfected at this point, featuring on several hits like '(Love Is Like A) Heatwave' by Martha Reeves & The Vandellas and 'My World Is Empty Without You' by The Supremes, giving the songs a raw, earthy grounding. The backing vocals are slightly different, however, as Otis Williams recalled in his memoirs that 'our vocal parts had been all switched around, so that I was singing a high second tenor, with Paul under me.'

Unusually for Temptations recordings, 'All I Need' also features additional backing vocals from Motown's female session group The Andantes. Comprised of Jackie Hicks, Marlene Barrow and Louvain Demps, the trio performed on many of the label's biggest hits, most prominently on almost all of the Four Tops' recordings, as well as providing the backing vocals for later Diana Ross & The Supremes recordings. They rarely featured on tracks by The Temptations, but here, their vocal blend gives a brighter, fuller vocal arrangement.

The track became a hit on both the US pop and R&B charts, reaching number two and eight, respectively. In classic Motown style, the song was covered by both The Supremes and Bobby Taylor, although both versions weren't released until 2005 and 2006, respectively.

'(Loneliness Made Me Realize) It's You That I Need' (Eddie Holland, Norman Whitfield)

Another Ruffin lead, this track was the last single to be released from *With A Lot O' Soul*, in September 1967, reaching number three on the R&B chart and number 14 on the pop chart; despite this, it would rarely be included on various 'Greatest Hits' packages later on. It also marks Eddie Holland's final collaboration with Norman Whitfield on a single. By 1968, Holland, along with his brother, Brian, and Lamont Dozier, quit Motown and began lengthy legal proceedings against Gordy for lack of payment, while starting their own company, encompassing the Hot Wax and Invictus labels.

The song is similar in its approach to 'Ain't No Sun Since You've Been Gone', although it's more of a mid-tempo ballad than a Motown stomper. The bass is mixed high, driving the song forward, while Whitfield deftly uses a string arrangement to sweeten the track. Ruffin delivers another fine vocal, singing the bulk of the song until the last verse, where each Temptation sings the line 'it's you that I need' in turn. Ruffin then takes control of the song as it reaches its climax, trying to replicate his approach on 'Ain't Too Proud To

Beg'. Although a hit at the time, looking back today, this one has unfortunately been forgotten in The Temptations' vast catalogue.

'No More Water In The Well' (Warren Moore, Smokey Robinson, Bobby Rogers)
This is the only song on the album to feature Paul Williams on lead vocals. Robinson certainly had a knack for writing and producing songs specifically for Williams: this is another breakup song, requiring the sort of emotional power and longing that Williams could deliver. Whether Robinson and his Miracles co-writers were influenced by William Bell's Stax classic 'You Don't Miss Your Water', which came out in 1961, or not, it certainly is reminiscent of it lyrically, although they deal with loss and grief in different ways. Both songs use water as a symbol of love: in 'No More Water In The Well', the narrator's woman has taken his love for granted and it's finally run out, whereas in Bell's song, he only realises he misses love once it's gone, and 'the well runs dry'.

Indeed, the lyrics feature some clever wordplay, by now expected from Robinson and his co-writers, particularly this section of the first verse, even with the repeated use of 'water':

> You take my love for granted like water
> Water you spill and you waste
> Though love is thicker than water
> It spills quicker than water

The rest of the group provide ad-libs later in the song, making for a particularly strong album cut, certainly much better than the early filler on their first albums.

'Save My Love For A Rainy Day' (Roger Penzabene, Norman Whitfield)
This is one of the earliest Temptations songs co-written by Roger Penzabene, a young songwriter and lyricist who could write both dreamy ballads and heart-achingly beautiful breakup songs, the latter of which he'd master a year later on 'I Wish It Would Rain'. He injected his feelings of his own turbulent relationship into his lyrics, writing frequently of loss and heartbreak, along with devotion to his wife. In this song, the narrator, played by Kendricks on lead, is struck by this woman's beauty like a 'lightning bolt', but she is, predictably, in love with someone else. The narrator, though, has plenty of time to wait, telling her to look him up once their love has ended and warning her that she's 'putting her heart in danger'.

It's certainly not as dark as later Penzabene lyrics and doesn't deviate from the standard Motown approach to ballads. Kendricks delivers another excellent lead, his voice soaring above the track and the backing vocals, sounding effortlessly cool in his attempt to woo back his love.

'Just One Last Look' (Brian Holland, Lamont Dozier, Eddie Holland)
A rare contribution from Holland-Dozier-Holland (H-D-H) for The Temptations – usually, their efforts were reserved for Four Tops and The Supremes – 'Just One Last Look' is another excellent forgotten Temptations track. The rhythm track is similar to Four Tops records of the time, with its pounding drumbeat, chunking guitars and prominent use of tambourine throughout, although Ruffin couldn't necessarily match Levi Stubbs for pure force in his lead vocals. (Four Tops would also record a version before H-D-H left Motown, though that was left unreleased until 2005.)

Nevertheless, Ruffin sings the lead and does a fine job playing the part of a jilted lover, with tears in his eyes, watching as his girl walks away, allowing himself just one last look at the girl who gave him so much happiness. In traditional H-D-H style, the sadness of the lyrics is hidden by both a powerful lead vocal and bright backing vocals, along with a mid-tempo, pounding groove – it's a formula that they'd perfected over their years as Motown's top hitmakers.

Despite the song's obvious greatness, it wasn't released as a single, presumably lost in the battle between Berry Gordy and H-D-H at the time, with the production trio demanding greater reward for their hit singles. Additionally, Whitfield no doubt was also keen to block any H-D-H single release with the group now that he had become their primary producer; he might let Frank Wilson record 'All I Need', but he was never going to be a serious threat to his hold over The Temptations. H-D-H, however, had a reputation as proven hitmakers and, had they produced a hit for The Temptations, history may well have repeated itself and Whitfield may have found himself replaced as the group's primary producer. These internal battles, then, meant that this song has largely gone unnoticed to the casual fan.

'Sorry Is A Sorry Word' (Eddie Holland, Ivy Jo Hunter)
The break-up songs keep coming on *With A Lot O' Soul*, with 'Sorry Is A Sorry Word' having Ruffin playing the part of a man whose girl has left him, telling him she's sorry – not something Ruffin is particularly pleased to hear – which fails to soften the blow. He questions how she could only feel sympathy for him 'after all the sweet love' he's given her, and implores her to remember him, although, surely, any woman would remember an encounter with David Ruffin. A pleasant if more forgettable effort than other album tracks here, it's nonetheless another virtuoso performance from Ruffin, no doubt adding to his ever-growing ego.

'You're My Everything' (Cornelius Grant, Roger Penzabene, Norman Whitfield)
Up until this point, although The Temptations were billed as a group with 'five lead singers', rarely did any single song feature a split lead between two or more members (though this would become more common once Ruffin had

been fired and replaced by Dennis Edwards). However, Whitfield tried something different on 'You're My Everything', splitting the lead vocals between Kendricks and Ruffin; the former sings lead in the first verse and the latter sings lead in the second. Indeed, the sweetness of Kendricks' tenor contrasts with the raspiness of Ruffin to create one of the group's finest ballads.

The song first began as a collaboration between Cornelius Grant and Roger Penzabene, two close friends who had grown up in the same neighbourhood. Grant told author and former Motown executive Adam White that he had first conceived of 'You're My Everything' as a showcase for Kendricks, feeling that he simply didn't get enough lead since the arrival of Ruffin, and that it was Kendricks, not Ruffin, who truly captivated the female audience during their concerts. Penzabene contributed the lyrics while Whitfield and Grant handled the music, with Grant also playing guitar on the track. Yet, given the impressive run of successful singles with Ruffin on lead, Whitfield clearly couldn't resist featuring him on lead either.

Unlike 'All I Need' or 'I Know (I'm Losing You)', there is no pleading for love and no begging for forgiveness; it's a straight-up love song, with lyrics not dissimilar to those early Smokey Robinson compositions, contrasting life before their relationship as 'dull and ordinary' with life now being 'sunny and bright'. This is emphasised by the summery, light pop feel of the backing track, something the group wouldn't revisit on future singles for the foreseeable future, particularly once Ruffin had left the group. But it was another top ten smash on both the R&B and pop charts (number three and six, respectively), showing that the group were more than simply just David Ruffin, even if that's what Ruffin himself was beginning to think.

'Now That You've Won Me' (Smokey Robinson)

This song first appeared in 1965 on Marvin Gaye's *How Sweet It Is To Be Loved By You* album. Gaye's version is a much sparser affair compared with the version presented on *With A Lot O' Soul,* with Robinson adding strings to this version to sweeten the track, matched by some equally sweet lead vocals by Ruffin and backing by the other Temptations.

Unlike much of the rest of the album, the lyrics deviate from the breakup theme; here, Ruffin tells his new love, now that she's 'won' him, to never change and remain the sweet girl he fell in love with. It has a mellow, laid-back groove, with some incredibly sweet strings combined with a soft, almost jazzy, horn arrangement. Like 'Sorry Is A Sorry Word', it's pleasant album filler, but is overshadowed by the album's singles.

'Two Sides To Love' (Sylvia Moy, Norman Whitfield)

The optimism of 'Now That You've Won Me' gives way to the pessimism of this Moy-Whitfield collaboration, in which love has once again broken down. Here, Kendricks is trying to convince a girl to love again after her relationship fails, telling her how glorious love can be – even better if she experiences it with him. It has a more doo-wop influence on the backing vocals, although Whitfield mixes the string arrangement in loudly, turning it into more of a pop song rather than pure soul. Kendricks sings a sweet lead, but Ruffin contributes a few ad-libs – presumably Whitfield requested them, or possibly Ruffin couldn't resist, not wanting to be outdone.

'Don't Send Me Away' (Eddie Kendricks, Smokey Robinson)
Although written by Kendricks and Robinson, it features a rare lead from Otis Williams, supported by Melvin Franklin. Williams has a fine voice, although compared with the power of Ruffin, the sweetness of Kendricks and the pure soul of Paul Williams, it's understandable why he didn't get more lead. His lead is not spectacular, but it's steady and warm, and the slow pace of the song suits his smooth tenor. On the few leads he has sung throughout his 60-plus years as a Temptation, the majority of them have been romantic ballads.

Of course, it wouldn't be a powerful enough performance for a single release (although it was the B-side to '(Loneliness Made Me Realize) It's You That I Need'), but it fills out the album and served to support Motown's claim that the group had 'five lead singers'.

In A Mellow Mood (1967)

Personnel:
Otis Williams, Melvin Franklin, Paul Williams, Eddie Kendricks, David Ruffin: vocals
The Funk Brothers: instrumentation
H.B Barnum, Oliver Nelson, Don Costa: arrangements
Produced at Hitsville USA, Detroit, by Frank Wilson and Jeffrey Bowen between April and October 1967
Label: Gordy
Release date: 27 November 1967
Length: 38:35
Charts: US R&B: 1

Four months after the release of *With A Lot O' Soul*, Motown issued *In A Mellow Mood*, a collection of tracks from the 'Great American Songbook' with jazzy, easy-listening arrangements. This was certainly a break from the soul the group had been recording up to this point, but this was a classic Berry Gordy move. Several of his top acts recorded similar albums of 'traditional pop' that sought to introduce the group to the white record-buying audience and the largely white patrons of the nation's supper clubs. These were venues where customers would usually enjoy dinner before some form of live entertainment. Such clubs included New York's Copacabana, where The Temptations, The Supremes and Marvin Gaye all appeared and recorded live albums. For a black musical act, playing these clubs could prove lucrative financially and would open more metaphorical doors than simply playing the venues that formed the 'Chitlin' Circuit', to which black artists were traditionally limited. Named after the soul food 'chitlins' (or 'chitterlings'), this was a term that referred to venues in the southern, eastern and mid-western areas of the US, where black artists were safe to perform, although the venue conditions varied.

Motown already employed this tactic with The Supremes, who had recorded an album titled *Sing Rodgers And Hart,* which featured their own covers of show tunes, including 'The Lady Is A Tramp' and 'My Funny Valentine'; not to be outdone, Four Tops recorded a similar album titled *On Broadway*, which included their own take on 'For Once In My Life' and 'My Way'. It was a calculated move to have Motown's top acts record such material, and it led, in part, to these groups playing the elite supper clubs, such as New York's Copacabana, where Marvin Gaye and The Supremes would record live albums, and eventually onto Las Vegas. In these shows, their hits were often condensed into medley form, while standards dominated the setlist. The Temptations recorded their own *Live At The Copa* album, which mixed their current hits with several selections from *In A Mellow Mood*, including 'For Once In My Life', 'The Impossible Dream' and 'With These Hands'. These sets served a purpose, and by the time the group recorded their next live album, *In Japan!*, these selections were no longer part of their repertoire.

Not all of The Temptations agreed with Gordy's plan to have them crossover to a new, whiter audience, however. Paul Williams was particularly sceptical about the move, fearing that such an album would alienate their core black audience, who were used to the harder-hitting R&B and mellow soul ballads of their earlier albums. Their new manager, Shelly Berger, however, argued that their current popularity meant that they could now take a chance in recording such an album, and that because it was a new product by The Temptations, many fans would buy the album regardless. His argument won the day, and *In A Mellow Mood* was recorded through the end of 1966 into 1967. It features some excellent vocals from the group, even if the arrangements themselves are largely uninspiring.

Neither Smokey Robinson nor Norman Whitfield was given the production duties this time around; while Whitfield had broken Robinson's stranglehold over the group, Gordy instead entrusted Frank Wilson and Jeffrey Bowen to produce, with arrangements from H.B Barnum, Oliver Nelson and Don Costa, who had worked extensively with Frank Sinatra. These experienced arrangers would guarantee the sound Gordy was looking for.

The album also featured a more equitable sharing of the leads, with Paul Williams, in particular, benefitting from this, giving several impressive performances, particularly on 'For Once In My Life', suiting the emotional depth of his baritone. Even Melvin Franklin was given a lead, recording 'Ol' Man River', giving him a signature song.

This would not be the group's only take at standards. In 1995, the group released *For Lover's Only*, a much more creative affair than *In A Mellow Mood*, and one of their best and most underrated albums. *In A Mellow Mood* is a pleasant, if not groundbreaking, album for The Temptations. These songs might have been more suited to the likes of Sinatra or Tony Bennett rather than the hottest male R&B group on the scene, but the album had a purpose to serve, and on those terms, it was a success. It proved that The Temptations were versatile singers who could handle any material put in front of them, and it sold enough to reach number one on the R&B chart.

'Hello Young Lovers' (Richard Rodgers, Oscar Hammerstein II)

In A Mellow Mood opens with 'Hello Young Lovers', a song written for the musical *The King & I* in 1951. It serves to introduce this new, different-sounding album, setting the scene for this selection of standards. It's a bouncy, jazzy rendition, on which the group sing the entire song in unison, with a few ad-libs thrown in by Ruffin towards the end, perhaps as a reminder that he was still the group's focal point. In the song's outro, as the group harmonise, each member gets their own moment to sing the line 'hello young lovers, wherever you are' solo, with the exception of Franklin.

It's a nice opening to the album and has been used as the opening number to their live set in recent years. They also weren't the only Motown act to cover this song: Stevie Wonder recorded a version for his 1969 album *My*

Cherie Amour, although his rendition is much more soulful with an R&B beat, almost unrecognisable from The Temptations' version.

'A Taste Of Honey' (Ric Marlow, Bobby Scott)

Written for the 1960 Broadway musical adaptation of the play *A Taste For Honey*, it was recorded as an instrumental by Herb Alpert and his Tijuana Brass band in 1965, winning him a Grammy. A vocal version was then created and recorded initially by Billy Dee Williams before being covered by The Beatles, Barbara Streisand, Tony Bennett and fellow Motown stars The Supremes and Four Tops on their 1971 album *The Magnificent Seven*.

The Temptations' version features a bold horn arrangement to open the song, and Kendricks takes the lead in the first and second verse, singing as sweet as honey, while the rest of The Temptations provide call-and-response backing, for example, in the first verse: 'Much sweeter than wine/(Don't you know honey's so much sweeter)'. As the song reaches its climax around the 1:40 mark, Ruffin steps in to once again vocalise and throw in some ad-libs, contrasting with Kendrick's smooth falsetto. If anything, it's a bit unnecessary, adding little to the final mix, other than to perhaps boost Ruffin's ego further into thinking all Temptations songs needed him to sing a piece of the lead for it to work.

'For Once In My Life' (Ron Miller, Orlando Murden)

Discovered by Berry Gordy in a piano bar in Chicago, Ron Miller was invited to join Motown as a songwriter, where, along with Orlando Murden, he wrote one of the label's most enduring songs, 'For Once In My Life'. According to *The Telegraph*, Miller wrote the lyrics to Murden's music after the birth of his first daughter. It was first recorded by Motown artist Connie Hains, but wasn't released (until 2015, at least, on the *Motown Unreleased 1965* compilation). Hains' time at Motown was short, and it's not clear why her version wasn't released, but presumably Motown didn't want it competing with the version Stevie Wonder was preparing. Indeed, Wonder's up-tempo version, complete with his harmonica playing, resulted in a massive US and UK pop hit for him in 1967.

However, it wasn't the first version to be released. Chess Records issued a version by Jean DuShon in 1966, yet it received virtually no airplay on the radio, and the resulting sales were poor. DuShon's manager, John Levy, claimed in his memoirs that Berry Gordy personally intervened to have it pulled from radio playlists, as he didn't want his rivals at Chess having a hit with what he considered a Motown song.

Although Wonder's version is fast-paced, Miller originally wrote it as a ballad – he had crooner Tony Bennett in mind when writing it – and it would be recorded in this way by The Temptations on *In A Mellow Mood*, giving Paul Williams one of his best leads as a Temptation. Williams' lead is deeply emotional, giving a gut-wrenching performance that overshadows almost every other performance on the album. The backing vocals are arranged so as not to overshadow Williams's performance, with Otis Williams doubling his very last line of the song. It would become one of Paul Williams' signature songs during the group's live performances, and would appear on both their *Live At The Copa* record and the soundtrack to their television special *TCB* with Diana Ross & The Supremes.

It's the *TCB* version that is the best of the three recorded; watching his performance on the special, you can see a man in both physical and emotional pain. Williams was not a well man, suffering from sickle cell anaemia, which was not helped by his growing dependency on alcohol. But his performance on *TCB* was probably his greatest as a Temptation, bringing himself almost to tears as the song concludes, a man emotionally spent. Later, when his performances became weaker, the group hired Richard Street, formerly of The Distants, to sing Williams' harmony parts from backstage, allowing him to save his voice for his big numbers: 'Don't Look Back' and 'For Once In My Life'.

The song would continue to be covered by both Motown artists, such as Martha Reeves & The Vandellas, Smokey Robinson & The Miracles and Four Tops, as well as non-Motown acts, including Frank Sinatra and Tony Bennett – the latter would sing it for the rest of his career in concert. Bennett also recorded a version with Stevie Wonder, which won them a Grammy in 2007.

'Somewhere' (Leonard Bernstein, Stephen Sondheim)

Opening with a cinematic string arrangement that swoops and soars, this version of 'Somewhere' is excellent. Taken from the musical *West Side Story,* Ruffin is given his first full lead vocal on *In A Mellow Mood*, beginning the song in a more restrained manner than usual, his vocal closely following the rising and falling pattern of the string arrangement in the first verse. It's not long, though, before he notches up his vocal, singing with his normal flamboyance, backed by some equally elegant vocals from the rest of the group. It's one of the better covers on *In A Mellow Mood*, thanks to both the dramatic string arrangement and Ruffin's lead vocal.

Interestingly, 'Somewhere' was a key part of The Supremes' live act at the Copacabana around this time, singing it both on *The Ed Sullivan Show* and *The Hollywood Palace* television show. It was recorded as part of an unreleased album titled *There's A Place For Us,* which Motown shelved – its premise was similar to *In A Mellow Mood*, featuring covers of classics and other American favourites. However, Motown instead released The Supremes' own album titled *Live At The Copa* (The Temptations and Marvin Gaye also released albums titled *Live At The Copa*). It was finally issued in 2004.

'Ol' Man River' (Jerome Kern, Oscar Hammerstein II)

Written for the 1927 musical *Show Boat*, the song became the most well-known from the show, and was recorded by the likes of Frank Sinatra, The Righteous

Brothers and even Sam Cooke. None of these versions, though, match The Temptations', which features a rare lead from Melvin Franklin. This version owes more to the original 1928 recording by Paul Robeson, another bass singer, but his version is far less dramatic than the one The Temptations recorded.

Their version begins acapella, with each of the other four Temptations singing a line, then all singing in unison before, dramatically, Franklin shouts his opening lines. The musical accompaniment then begins, starting with just guitars and bass, and some incredibly tight harmonies, before Franklin begins his lead proper. He begins restrained, but his deep voice is a wonder to behold and suits the subject matter of the song perfectly.

Since it was first written, the lyrics have been changed on later recordings to make it more suitable to modern audiences. In The Temptations' version, the lines:

> Niggers all work on de Mississippi,
> Niggers all work while de white folks play…

Were replaced by:

> Here we all work on the Mississippi
> Here we all work while the rich boys play

Although written by Kern and Hammerstein, the song deals with the African-American experience in the early 20th century; the hardships, the poor treatment and back-breaking work that many were forced to endure are contrasted with the never-ending flow of the Mississippi. As The Temptations' version reaches the memorable line 'I'm tired of living, but 'fraid of dying, but ol' man river he just keeps rollin' along', the group sing acapella once again before it ends.

Franklin's performance here is one of the finest. It's no wonder the group began calling him 'the world's greatest bass singer'. Indeed, 'Ol' Man River' became his signature song and a staple of their setlists for decades to come, and live versions appear on *Temptations Live!* and *Live At The Copa*. For Franklin, it was an important performance to him personally, telling author Gerri Hershey:

> When we got into 'Old Man River' and the audience stood up, tears were in my eyes. I was trembling. Then, the other guys had to hold me 'cause I was trembling and it was beautiful. From the first moment I opened my mouth, I felt I was in my place in the universe.

'I'm Ready For Love' (Brian Holland, Lamont Dozier, Eddie Holland)
Not a standard or a number from a recent musical, 'I'm Ready For Love' is a Holland-Dozier-Holland song, originally written for Motown's Martha Reeves

& The Vandellas and which was released as a single in 1966. Here, given Reeves' own powerful lead, naturally, Ruffin takes the reins and delivers an equally forceful lead vocal.

To fit with the rest of the album, the arrangement is given a big-band makeover. It's got a big, brassy arrangement and a rhythm track that bounces along breezily thanks to the energetic bass playing. A driving hi-hat provides a distinctly jazz feel and the group provide backing vocals that wouldn't sound amiss on a Broadway cast album. There's a saxophone solo two-thirds through the track, accompanied by handclaps, which is less gritty than the R&B-style saxophone solos usually favoured on Motown songs, such as those by Junior Walker. Instead, this solo swings and is more melodic, albeit short, fading back into the arrangement.

'Try To Remember' (Tom Jones, Harvey Schmidt)
As the first song in the musical *The Fantasticks,* 'Try To Remember' is a nostalgic affair in which the narrator urges the audience to remember 'when life was so tender'. Listening today, the lyrics are a little old-fashioned, but in the hands of Kendricks on lead, it achieves the desired nostalgic effect, even if Kendricks, a young man in his mid-20s, is singing about how good things were back in the old days. Nevertheless, it's suitably sentimental, helped along by some incredibly dreamy backing harmonies (especially when they harmonise on 'follow, follow, follow!'), accompanied by a dream-like string arrangement.

'Who Can I Turn To (When Nobody Needs Me)' (Leslie Bricusse, Anthony Newley)
The album takes a turn away from being positively sentimental to more negative with this cover of 'Who Can I Turn To'. Given the depressing lyrics and the brooding arrangement, it's no surprise that Paul Williams was given the lead vocal here, delivering his trademark mournful baritone to create something really rather sad. It's certainly gloomier than the more popular version by Tony Bennett, but the backing vocals make it a more creative cover than other versions. This is particularly true when the rest of The Temptations harmonise in the bridge, replying to Paul Williams, singing 'Now listen here, Paul, don't you worry, maybe tomorrow you'll find what you're after'. Paul repeats this in his speaking voice before continuing to sing the final lines into the song's climax. Given his own personal struggles and later suicide, it's a prophetic choice of song, almost as if this song was written for him.

'What Now My Love' (Gilbert Bécaud, Pierre Delanoë, Carl Sigman)
Adapted into English from French by Carl Sigman, 'What Now My Love' has been covered over 400 times, from the likes of Shirley Bassey to Elvis Presley, who performed it live on his television special *Aloha From Hawaii*. Given the sheer number of recordings of the song, The Temptations' version is just that:

another version. The vocals are predictably excellent, with Melvin Franklin even trying his best at speaking French in the song's introduction, and the arrangement is almost cinematic in its climax. But it's less dramatic than other songs on *In A Mellow Mood*, and even with Ruffin on the lead, it's one of the more forgettable covers.

'That's Life' (Dean Kay, Kelly Gordon)
First recorded by Marion Montgomery in 1963, it was Frank Sinatra who turned it into a classic three years later. The Temptations' version on *In A Mellow Mood* doesn't quite reach the same stratospheric levels as ol' blue eyes, which is not helped by the slightly faster tempo, giving the impression that the group are rushing through it, lacking the depth that arranger Nelson Riddle gave the Sinatra version.

This is a shame as Paul Williams sings lead here, and with a slower, more subdued arrangement like he had on 'For Once In My Life', he would have undoubtedly given a better, more memorable performance. That said, the song's lyrics about the ups and downs of life (and, in his case, fame) suited Williams and all that he was going through personally. The backing vocals are arranged to respond in parts to Williams, which might work on an R&B stomper, but seems a bit disjointed here, giving it the feeling of a cabaret act. Ruffin ad-libs towards the end of the song, which distracts a bit from Williams's lead, but that, too, also lacks the punch Sinatra was able to give.

'With These Hands' (Benny Davis, Abner Silver)
First released in 1953 by Eddie Fisher, both Shirley Bassey and Tom Jones had hits with 'With These Hands' before The Temptations had their turn. Kendricks takes the lead here, giving another fine performance, reaching the high notes with ease. The group also provide more impressive harmonies, as they sing the chorus in unison before Kendricks resumes the lead. It's a perfectly pleasant cover, although it lacks the bite and power of others on the album.

'The Impossible Dream' (Joe Darion, Mitch Leigh)
In A Mellow Mood closes with 'The Impossible Dream' from the musical *Man Of La Mancha*. Frank Sinatra included a version on his album *That's Life* in 1966, and as good as that cover is, David Ruffin certainly gives the Chairman of the Board a run for his money on The Temptations' excellent version. For one, Sinatra didn't have the benefit of having the incredibly gorgeous backing vocals of The Temptations. Yet, the focus is purely on Ruffin's lead vocal, and he truly owns the song, as if he's singing about his own seemingly impossible dream of a poor black boy wanting and becoming both a singer and a star.

It would become part of the group's live repertoire, even after Ruffin was fired from the group. A live version appears on the group's *Live At London's Talk Of The Town* album in 1970, but this time with Dennis Edwards on lead, who delivers a powerful, although less nuanced, lead.

The Temptations Wish It Would Rain (1968)

Personnel:
Otis Williams, Melvin Franklin, Paul Williams, Eddie Kendricks, David Ruffin: vocals
The Funk Brothers: instrumentation
Produced at Hitsville USA, Detroit, by Norman Whitfield, Smokey Robinson, Henry Cosby, Dennis Lussier, Harvey Fuqua, Johnny Bristol, James Dean and William Weatherspoon between February 1967 and February 1968
Label: Gordy
Release date: 29 April 1968
Length: 31:32
Charts: US pop: 13, US R&B: 1

Almost four years to the date that Motown first released *Meet The Temptations*, the group were preparing to fire David Ruffin. *Wish It Would Rain* would mark his final performances as a Temptation until the *Reunion* album in 1982, although his contributions to that album were minimal. Here, though, *Wish It Would Rain* is one of the group's most introspective efforts, full of plaintive gut-wrenching heartbreak songs, led by the poignant title track. If anything, the album was the perfect send-off for Ruffin, symbolising the internal struggles of the group and foreshadowing the further internal strife just a few years later.

Berry Gordy later wrote in his memoir that the situation between Ruffin and the others had simply become untenable by 1968:

> [T]he Tempts' essential quality was that they were a tight, precise, perfectly synchronised unit. The five moved as one body. David was threatening that unity.

That, though, might have been looking back with a somewhat sanitised view. Unlike their label mates, Four Tops, who were genuinely friends and were able to go almost four decades without a personnel change (and even then, only because of illness and death), The Temptations had bickered throughout their time at Motown. On one side, Otis Williams and Melvin Franklin would usually side together, Paul Williams would usually be in the middle of things, while Kendricks and Ruffin complained about their treatment by Motown, combined with Ruffin's ever-growing ego, which was constantly fed by the people he surrounded himself with, hanging onto his coattails. Yet, they persisted, fearful that any change in the group's personnel might be the end of the group. Ruffin, of course, knew that they weren't going to risk that and saw no need to change his behaviour, believing himself to be bigger than the group.

In Mark Riboswky's biography of the group, he quotes the group's then-manager, Don Foster, who said that after the group's initial success of 'My Girl', it was clear Ruffin was going to cause the group serious trouble. Added to the mix was his increasing drug use, and relations were not happy between the members of the group. He also suggested, unwisely, that because he was the group's prime lead singer, they should be renamed 'David Ruffin & The Temptations'. After all, the Supremes had become Diana Ross & The Supremes as had Smokey Robinson & The Miracles, not to mention Martha Reeves & The Vandellas or Gladys Knight & The Pips. For the rest of the group, though, changing their name was a non-starter. With that, the die was cast.

The final decision to fire Ruffin came during a residency in Cleveland in June 1968: with two shows left, Ruffin went missing, deciding it was more fun to party with Dean Martin's daughter than carry out his contractual obligations. When he did show up, in the middle of one of the shows, to a resounding applause, the others hid their anger until the show was over – and the decision was made. Later, it was claimed that Otis Williams made the decision alone, something he refuted several times, making it clear that it was, however reluctantly, a group decision.

Therefore, *Wish It Would Rain* became Ruffin's swan song, a brilliant last album from the 'Classic Five' lineup. The songs reflected the album's title, with a focus on sadder songs, centred around variations of breakups and heartache. It was also more of a collaborative effort between several producers, rather than just Norman Whitfield, although he did produce the bulk of the tracks. But with Ruffin's departure and the hiring of Dennis Edwards to replace him, Whitfield took full control for the next eight albums.

There would, of course, be plenty of Temptations lineups to come, but none could encapsulate or even accurately mimic the sound that these five men had. As Otis Williams himself wrote later:

> No matter how you measure it, the lineup of Melvin, Eddie, David, Paul and me had a special magic that can never be recreated or recaptured.

'I Could Never Love Another (After Loving You)' (Roger Penzabene, Barrett Strong, Norman Whitfield)

The song, released as a single in April 1968, is essentially the follow-up to 'I Wish It Would Rain': in that song, the narrator cannot get over the shock of his relationship ending, and in this song, he still is unable to get over the loss, declaring himself unable to love again. The song features one of the final sets of lyrics written by Penzabene before his suicide on New Year's Eve 1967. It was, of course, all based on Penzabene's own breakup and subsequent depression.

Ruffin sings the lead, his final lead to be released as a single before his departure from the group. The track opens with percussion, sounding like a horse galloping, before the melancholy strings and guitar strumming fade in. The strings are particularly emotive, mixed relatively low, but conveying a sense of misery and pain. The backing vocals, too, are fairly restrained, placing the emphasis on Ruffin's phenomenal lead vocal; he pleads, hollers and growls his way through Penzabene's intensely personal lyrics (although the line 'taken away my reason for living' may have been pinched from Four Tops' 'Standing In The Shadows Of Love'). Ruffin certainly plays the part of the jilted lover well, using all his vocal trickery and mastery to do justice to the song and its context.

It was another hit, reaching the top spot on the R&B chart and number 13 on the pop chart.

'Cindy' (Smokey Robinson)

The breakup songs continue with 'Cindy', written and produced by Smokey Robinson, who gives Ruffin the lead. Not as strong as the Whitfield-Strong-Penzabene songs, it's nevertheless decent for an album track, helped by Ruffin's powerful lead, on which he pleads for Cindy to return, as the rest of The Temptations ask in the choruses, 'When will you come home, Cindy?' Franklin is particularly prominent in the vocal mix, but once again, the focus is all on Ruffin.

Bobby Taylor also recorded a version during his stint at Motown, but it was kept in the vault until 2002. Similarly, crooner Bobby Darin also recorded a version during his short stint signed to Motown in the early 1970s, which was produced by Robinson and featured him on vocals.

'I Wish It Would Rain' (Roger Penzabene, Barrett Strong, Norman Whitfield)

One of Ruffin's truly defining performances, 'I Wish It Would Rain' was the first single to be released from the album in December 1967. It was another collaboration between Strong and Whitfield and Roger Penzabene, with the latter providing the lyrics. Whitfield and Strong had first recorded the basic backing tracks in April 1967 and had planned on giving the song to Jimmy Ruffin, David's brother, instead, but by late summer, when they were collecting material for The Temptations, Penzabene had written a new set of poetic, if deeply sad, lyrics.

The song drew from Penzabene's own personal life and, in particular, his troubled relationship with his wife after he allegedly found out she was cheating on him. Heartbroken, he poured his angst into this and 'I Could Never Love Another (After Loving You)'. The narrator on 'I Wish It Would Rain' simply wishes the weather would match his own internal frame of mind: he desires rainfall in order to hide the tears his woman has caused, but unfortunately for him, it's always 'such a lovely day'. The lyrics are almost Smokey Robinson-esque, pitting the narrator's emotional state against the glorious weather outside, contrasting the light and the dark. According to Graham Betts in his epic *Motown Encyclopaedia,* Penzabene was present the day that Ruffin recorded his lead vocal; his performance was almost too much for him to bear, spending most of the session in the control booth crying.

The song opens mournfully with just Ruffin harmonising, accompanied by piano, before the other Temptations come in with the backing. The piano drives the song in the first verse before the rest of the Funk Brothers and strings come in on the second, as Ruffin becomes more and more emotional. In the first verse, Whitfield even mixes in the sounds of seagulls squawking, giving the track an eerie quality. As Ruffin sings 'Let it rain, rain, rain!', the group harmonise behind him, 'Oh, how I wish that it would rain'. The harmonies are somewhat brighter than Ruffin's yearning lead, but the focus is on Ruffin.

Clearly the best song recorded for what would become *I Wish It Would Rain*, it was released as a single just before Christmas 1967, although Penzabene wouldn't live long enough to see it become one of the group's biggest hits. It eventually went to number one on the R&B charts and hit number four on the pop charts (even hitting number 45 on the UK singles chart), but Penzabene committed suicide on New Year's Eve, unable to manage his depression.

The song was also nominated for a Grammy for Best R&B Song, although they predictably lost out to Otis Redding, who won posthumously with '(Sitting On) The Dock Of The Bay'. Whitfield, ever the avid recycler of material, recorded the song again in 1968 with Gladys Knight & The Pips; their version was also a hit on the R&B charts, reaching number 15, before Marvin Gaye also recorded a version for his Whitfield-produced album *That's The Way Love Is*. They weren't the only ones to cover the song either: Bobby Womack had a go, The Faces had a UK hit with their cover, Aretha Franklin recorded it on her Luther Vandross-produced album *Get It Right* and even Bruce Springsteen recorded it for his 2022 album *Only The Strong Survive*.

The same story – standing in the rain to hide tears after a breakup – was used on The Dramatics' 'In The Rain' in 1972 by writer Tony Hester.

'Please Return Your Love To Me' (Norman Whitfield, Barrett Strong, Barbara Neely)

The third single from *Wish It Would Rain*, and released after Ruffin's departure, it was presumably chosen as it featured Kendricks on lead rather than Ruffin. Indeed, it's Kendricks' first solo lead on a single since 'Get Ready' (excluding 'You're My Everything', on which he shared lead with Ruffin). The song carries on the same theme of the first three songs: Kendricks' girl has left him, leaving him sad and lonely, and he begs, albeit in a sweeter fashion than Ruffin, for her to return her love. Unlike the Penzabene lyrics, though, the narrator here is in the wrong, asking the girl to 'forgive me for the wrong I've done'. With Kendricks utilising his delicate falsetto, what woman could resist such a request?

The arrangement is somewhat brighter and lighter than the previous singles released with Ruffin on lead and the string arrangement, in particular, sounds much more breezy and slightly odd, given that the song isn't a ballad. But it's another fine single, and although it was a more modest hit than 'I Wish It Would Rain', it still managed to reach number four on the R&B chart and number 23 on the pop chart. It was backed by the Paul Williams-led 'How Can I Forget', which wasn't included on *Wish It Would Rain* and was eventually included on their *Emperors Of Soul* box set in 1994.

'Fan The Flame' (Al Cleveland, Terry Johnson, Smokey Robinson)
The first song on *Wish It Would Rain* to feature a horn arrangement, 'Fan The Flame' has yet another lead by Ruffin. One of the better album cuts on *Wish It Would Rain*, it hints at the direction that 1970s soul would take with its smooth groove and more polished feel. There's room for a bold horn arrangement, including some mellow flute playing in the background in the second verse.

The song is a manual for men about love, providing handy instructions for the male listener on how to 'fan the flame' of love, placing special emphasis on the 'little things that mean a lot'. The key, though, is to 'keep it burning hot', something doubtless Ruffin always did. One peculiar lyric, though, probably hasn't dated as well: 'A woman lives on vanity, so fan the flames'. That aside, it's decent album filler material, helped yet again by the impassioned vocal from Ruffin.

'He Who Picks A Rose' (Eddie Holland, Emilio Smiley, Norman Whitfield)
Funkier than the rest of *Wish It Would Rain*, Ruffin romps through 'He Who Picks A Rose', a Motown jam that uses imagery of flowers to convey the beauty of a woman. It draws on Marv Johnson's 'I'll Pick A Rose For My Rose', although this song is much faster paced. Again, it contains some advice for the male listener, telling them that 'you have to take the bitter with the sweet' – a relationship isn't always smooth sailing:

> Remember, they're not perfect you see,
> So you got to take the bitter with the sweet,
> And remember fellas, he who picks a rose,
> Must accept the thorns it bear

Although this version was the first to be released, Whitfield had already recorded the song initially with David's brother Jimmy in 1967, but it would sit in the Motown vault until 2001. Edwin Starr also recorded a version, as did Rare Earth in 1969 and 1976, respectively. The song found some fame on the UK's 'Northern Soul' scene when a version by The Carstairs was found, originally released in 1969.

'Why Did You Leave Me Darling' (James Dean, Deke Richards)
The pleading 'oh-why-did-you-leave-me' songs make a comeback here. Like so many Motown songs, the despairing lyrics are masked by an up-tempo

beat and plenty of percussion, making it almost a dance number, even if Ruffin is singing about some serious heartbreak. Indeed, Ruffin rips his way through the song at a frantic pace, nearly shouting the lyrics, screaming at the girl in the song, begging to know why she's left him. His delivery is so fast that it feels like the rest of the group are struggling to keep up with his shouting and growling; it's certainly an epic performance from Ruffin, and somewhat ominously foreshadows the approach his replacement, Dennis Edwards, would take when he joined the group, with him able to sing at such speed and force.

'I Truly, Truly Believe' (George Gordy, Margaret Gordy, Allen Story)
Co-written by Berry Gordy's siblings George and Margaret, along with another Motown songwriter, Allen Story, 'I Truly, Truly Believe' is somewhat of a throwback to the more innocent love songs rather than the breakup songs that dominate the rest of the album. It features a rare lead for Melvin Franklin, which, alongside 'Ol' Man River', became one of his signature songs in concert; a live version appeared on the *Live At The Copa* album, released later in 1968.

Franklin's voice thunders, like a storm brewing, but somehow his deep voice seduces thanks to the soft, romantic lyrics. To counter Franklin's low rumbles, the backing vocals feature Kendricks prominently, acting as a counterbalance. The instrumentation is sparse, but there is a nice guitar solo and a somewhat muted horn section in the choruses. It's certainly not as strong as the singles released from *Wish It Would Rain*, but it's one of the finer album cuts here.

'This Is My Beloved' (Nickolas Ashford, Valerie Simpson)
One of the few Ashford and Simpson tracks the group recorded, 'This Is My Beloved' is a sweet ballad featuring Kendricks on lead, another contrast to the more depressing numbers on the rest of the album. Its lyrics tell the story of a guy whose girl makes him 'feel ten feet tall'; the narrator never mentions her beauty, only how supportive she is of him, which, in turn, makes the narrator more vulnerable than he sounds. It's the kind of sophisticated soul that Ashford and Simpson perfected at Motown, and hints at what they could have achieved with The Temptations if they'd been given a chance.

'Gonna Give Her All The Love I've Got' (Norman Whitfield, Barrett Strong)
First recorded by Jimmy Ruffin in 1967, it was a significant hit for him, reaching the top 30 on the pop chart and an impressive number 14 on the R&B chart. Here, though, it's not brother David who sings the lead; instead, Paul Williams gets his first of two leads on *Wish It Would Rain*. The song is sung from the perspective of a recently released prisoner who, with his newfound freedom, is returning to his girl to give her 'all the love I've got'

(although it could also perhaps be interpreted as a soldier returning from war – but the line about him sitting next to his window suggests not).

The song opens with bass notes that sound like they were pinched straight from Frankie Valli & The Four Seasons' hit 'Rag Doll', which repeat throughout the first verse; Williams and the rest of The Temptations are accompanied only by the bass until the first chorus, when the rest of the Funk Brothers join in. It's not the finest of leads from Williams, who tries his best, as he struggles to convey the same emotional depth as his vocals on 'Don't Look Back' or 'For Once In My Life'.

Unsurprisingly, Whitfield also recorded this with Marvin Gaye in 1970, and it was also released as a single but was only a minor hit.

'I've Passed This Way Before' (James Dean, William Weatherspoon)

Another song about heartbreak, Franklin opens the song up with a spoken-word introduction, declaring that 'life lands a crushing blow, and once again a heart is broken … a hurt that took so long to end, has found my poor heart again'. Setting a suitably depressing scenario, Franklin gives way to yet another Ruffin lead vocal, as he picks up the story, reminiscing about the old memories of heartache from a previous love. Similar to 'This Is My Beloved', the narrator reveals a vulnerable side, although it's more explicit here, with Ruffin claiming that, without love, a man 'walks in the dark, baby'.

Like 'Gonna Give Her All I've Got', this song was first released as a single by Ruffin's brother, Jimmy, who had a number-17 pop hit with it in America, and it peaked at number 29 on the UK singles chart. It no doubt made sense to record such a pleading song with Jimmy, given his success with 'What Becomes Of A Brokenhearted', and this single, when released in the UK in 1969, saw a resurgence in his career, at least in the UK.

'No Man Can Love Her Like I Do' (Eddie Holland, Norman Whitfield, Eddie Kendricks)

The last song on the album also features the last writing contribution from Kendricks on a song recorded by the group. However, it is Paul Williams who does the honours on lead vocals, and he is more effective here than on 'Gonna Give Her All The Love I've Got'. The backing vocals are very high, and although not listed on the album, it's possible the Andantes were brought into the studio to sweeten the arrangement.

The song is a classic Motown stomper, showcasing a fierce beat, excellent vocals and a saxophone solo before the final verse. Lyrically, it's a simple song about a guy who believes no-one can love his girl like he can, again something of a throwback to earlier Motown songs.

Cloud Nine (1969)

Personnel:
Otis Williams, Melvin Franklin, Paul Williams, Eddie Kendricks, Dennis Edwards: vocals
The Funk Brothers: instrumentation
Produced at Hitsville USA, Detroit, by Norman Whitfield between July 1967 and December 1968
Label: Gordy
Release date: 17 February 1969
Length: 34:35
Charts: US Pop: 4, US R&B: 1, UK: 32

Replacing David Ruffin was always going to be a difficult task for The Temptations, but their decision to hire Dennis Edwards was a masterstroke. Born in Fairfield, Alabama, Edwards began singing, like so many soul stars, in a church where his father, Reverend Dennis Edwards Senior, preached. The family moved north by the time Edwards was ten. He ended up singing in the gospel group The Mighty Clouds of Joy and studied music at the Detroit Conservatory of Music. Like his hero Sam Cooke, he soon crossed the line into secular music, forming his own group, Dennis Edwards & The Fireballs, singing a mixture of soul and jazz. After a period in the US Army, he eventually came across bassist James Jamerson of Motown's famed Funk Brothers and wound up auditioning for Motown. Placed on a retainer, he was drafted into The Contours when their singer, Billy Gordon, fell ill. Fate intervened, and soon the group began opening shows for The Temptations, where the group became interested in this new singer, while their own lead singer became more erratic and estranged.

As Otis Williams wrote in his autobiography, Edwards could handle the songs Ruffin sang lead on, while also giving the group a new sound. He wasn't necessarily as soulful as Ruffin, but he had an unmatched intensity to his voice, which suited the new material that Norman Whitfield and Barrett Strong were writing. *Cloud Nine* was the first studio album to feature Edwards as a Temptation, but he had already appeared on their *Live At The Copa* album, released in December 1968, as well as the albums the group recorded with Diana Ross & The Supremes, *Diana Ross & The Supremes Join The Temptations* (released in November 1968) and the live album *TCB* (released in December 1968) from their NBC television special. But it was *Cloud Nine* where Edwards came into his own.

The arrival of Edwards coincided with a new sound for The Temptations, which Williams dubbed 'psychedelic soul'. According to Williams, he told Whitfield to listen to recent Sly & The Family Stone records, particularly their hit 'Dance To The Music', figuring that this new style of funk could work for The Temptations, particularly the sharing of lyrics between different members of the group. On Williams' account, Whitfield was at first dismissive, saying

Right: The Supremes, The Miracles, The Temptations & Martha and the Vandellas in London in March 1965. (*Alamy*)

Below: David Ruffin of The Temptations with Diana Ross and The Supremes in rehearsal for *The Ed Sullivan Show* in 1967.

Left: Dressed as soldiers after a desert battle, *Wish It Would Rain* (1968) would be the last full Temptations album to feature David Ruffin. (*Gordy/Motown*)

Right: The Temptations enter their 'psychedelic-soul' era with *Cloud Nine* (1969). (*Gordy/Motown*)

Left: The album cover for *Puzzle People* (1969), with the group dressed in funky threads. (*Gordy/Motown*)

Right: Whitfield continued with his own brand of psychedelia on *Psychedelic Shack* (1970), which featured the first version of 'War'. (*Gordy/Motown*)

Left: *Sky's The Limit* (1971) was the last full album to feature Paul Williams and Eddie Kendricks. (*Gordy/Motown*)

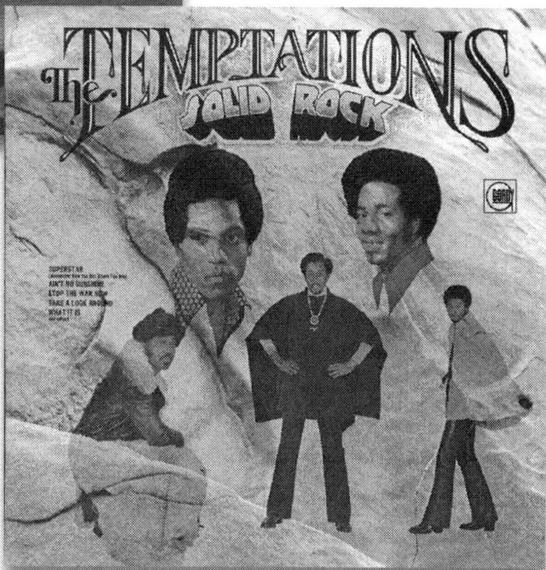

Right: New members Damon Harris and Richard Street loom large on the cover of *Solid Rock* (1972). (*Gordy/Motown*)

Above: The Temptations circa 1974: Richard Street, Otis Williams, Melvin Franklin, Dennis Edwards and Damon Harris. (*Getty*)

that it was nothing more than a mere fad, yet a few weeks later, returned to present the group with the song 'Cloud Nine', a futuristic slice of funk, different to anything the group had recorded before, drawing inspiration from Sly Stone, but with a Motown twist.

Cloud Nine was also part of a new musical direction for Motown, which, until then, hadn't largely dealt with overtly political and social issues (although, a year earlier, Diana Ross & The Supremes had a major hit with 'Love Child', a song about a child born out of wedlock and living in poverty in the inner city). Gordy had long subscribed to his 'KISS' mantra: keep it simple, stupid. While the music itself became more sophisticated in the later part of the decade, Gordy was aware that political statements from black artists had the potential to alienate white music buyers, especially after the label had put so much effort into cultivating them. Yet, for Whitfield at least, the decision to write and record more politically orientated material was primarily economic. Otis Williams told Dorian Lynsky in her book that he couldn't remember Whitfield being that political and couldn't recall him ever talking about current affairs. 'That's just what was happening in the world at the time', he told Lynskey, 'Norman and Barrett decided to capitalise on what was happening.' Regardless, though, the songs worked and set the direction for The Temptations in the years to come, moving away from the love songs they'd previously been associated with.

The album isn't all political, though: side one features the new, gritty soul of 'Cloud Nine' and 'Runaway Child, Running Wild', but the rest of the album contains songs more fitting with their usual material, a combination of up-tempo numbers and ballads. And, like so many of their albums to date, several of these 'filler' tracks were recorded by other Motown artists and written in-house. But it's those two singles that dominate the album and set the musical direction for The Temptations for the next several years.

'Cloud Nine' (Norman Whitfield, Barrett Strong)

A rapid departure from the group's previous sound, the arrival of Dennis Edwards gave Whitfield both the voice and the opportunity to modernise their sound. Williams recalled in his memoir that while the group were now largely prevented from writing their own material, like they had done in the early days, they still tried to get their 'two cents' in when it came to decisions about what they were recording. After all, it was their career on the line.

As a result, at least according to Williams, the impetus for 'Cloud Nine' came from him encouraging Whitfield to listen to what Sly & The Family Stone were doing out on the East Coast, particularly their infectious groove 'Dance To The Music'. Stone combined R&B, rock and psychedelia to create his own brand of hippy-funk, all played by a racially integrated band. Whitfield, though, at first, wasn't convinced of Stone's new sound, declaring it to be nothing more than 'a little passing fancy'. But by the time Whitfield summoned the group a few weeks later to Hitsville, he and Strong had written 'Cloud Nine'.

Opening with wah-wah guitars, a thumping bassline and some incredibly tight drumming matched by the tight harmonies, 'Cloud Nine' sounds unlike any other previous Temptations song. Like 'Dance To The Music', the lead vocals are shared out, with Edwards attacking the first verse with an intensity no other Temptation, before or since, has been able to match. He shares the lead with Paul Williams, who takes the second verse, before returning for the third verse, where he's practically shouting the lyrics. He then trades lines with Paul Williams and Kendricks, as the track pounds along. Kendricks' dreamy falsetto is contrasted by both Edwards and Franklin, who contribute a line.

The song marked the first session that guitarist Dennis Coffey played on for Motown. Coffey brought a new set of tricks for the guitarists at Motown, using much more distortion when playing to give a more psychedelic sound, along with his use of tape-loop delays and wah-wah pedals, which would feature even more prominently on future Whitfield productions. Overall, the group were pleased: they'd successfully navigated the firing of Ruffin and had a new hit on their hands.

However, Berry Gordy, ever conscious of alienating the white people who bought Motown's records in their thousands, was unsure of both the new sound and the lyrics Strong had come up with. On the face of it, the lyrics are clearly about drug usage; the first verse describes how the narrator's 'childhood part of my life wasn't very pretty', that it was 'hard times', and he 'needed something to ease my troubled mind'. Once this 'something' was taken or had, the narrator is now 'doing fine, up here on Cloud Nine'. In his memoir, Otis Williams wrote, somewhat unconvincingly:

> Contrary to popular belief, the song is not about drugs – Norman didn't do drugs – but about changing your attitude internally, no matter how impossible that might seem. The lyrics even admit that the 'world of love and harmony' is a 'million miles from reality'.

Of course, this wasn't explicit in Strong's lyrics, nor did he or Whitfield explain how someone could change their mindset, even in a hopeless situation. Despite Gordy's misgivings, though, 'Cloud Nine' was a huge hit for the group: it peaked at number two on the R&B charts and number six on the pop chart when released in October 1968, and the following year, it was the first Motown song to win a Grammy. The Temptations won for 'Best R&B Performance by a Duo or Group with Vocals', beating out competition from Sam & Dave, Peggy Scott and Jo Jo Benson, The Sweet Inspirations and Archie Bell & The Drells.

'I Heard It Through The Grapevine' (Norman Whitfield, Barrett Strong)
Written by Whitfield and Strong back in 1966, it was first recorded by The Miracles, although their version wouldn't appear until 1968 as an album track on their *Special Occasion* album. Next, Whitfield gave it to Marvin Gaye,

although according to Graham Betts, author of *Motown Encyclopaedia*, the instrumental tracks were originally meant for The Temptations. Whitfield clearly changed his mind and forced Gaye to sing in a higher key than he was comfortable with (similar to the way he made David Ruffin sing 'Ain't Too Proud To Beg', and he would employ the tactic again on Gaye's 'Too Busy Thinking About My Baby'), consequently creating one of Motown's best recordings. Yet, it was blocked by release from Berry Gordy, arguing that Gaye needed a romantic single instead. Whitfield, riled up, then cut a gospel-infused version with Gladys Knight & The Pips, which was released as a single, selling a million copies, and was nominated for a Grammy. Eventually, Gordy caved in and Gaye's version was released, outselling Gladys Knight & The Pips' version.

Whether Whitfield felt he could have another hit version of the song is unknown, but it no doubt made sense to have The Temptations record it for *Cloud Nine,* even if it was just purely financial in boosting Whitfield and Strong's publishing.

The Temptations' version, though, owes much to the Gladys Knight & The Pips' version, lacking that dark, brooding quality that made Gaye's version so special. The arrangement is an interesting choice, given that Edwards had a more powerful voice than Gaye, and no doubt could have handled a more intense rhythm arrangement. Perhaps that was too obvious for Whitfield, who chose to rearrange the track to highlight the group's harmonies instead. The group sing the first five lines of the first verse in harmony before Edwards takes the lead and rips through the last two lines, leading into the chorus. He then sings lead on the chorus, with the others providing call-and-response vocals, similar to the Pips. In the second verse, the pattern is repeated, but this time, Kendricks picks the lead up into the chorus.

The Temptations' version is pleasant enough, but it pales in comparison to those by Gladys Knight & The Pips and Marvin Gaye; the arrangement isn't good enough to compete. 'Grapevine', however, went on to be one of the most covered Motown songs of all, with a diverse range of artists recording it, from Ella Fitzgerald to Vanilla Fudge to Roger Troutman of the Zapp Band.

'Runaway Child, Running Wild' (Norman Whitfield, Barrett Strong)
He might have been ambivalent about Sly Stone's productions at first, but Whitfield couldn't deny his influence on this song, an almost ten-minute-long track that pushed The Temptations even further away from their usual sound. Other acts were beginning to push the limit when it came to album tracks, increasing their length, but this was largely unheard of at Motown, especially on one of the label's top acts. Yet, Whitfield was unperturbed, willing to push the limits of what Gordy and his executives would accept. Given his track record, he could afford to experiment.

What he created on 'Runaway Child, Running Wild' is a cinematic tale of a young boy who leaves the safety and comfort of his home after skipping school; 'frightened and afraid', he loses himself in an unknown, dangerous world, with the voices in his head – The Temptations' backing vocals – telling him that 'you better go back home, where you belong'. As the song comes to a climax, the hi-hat drumming intensifies as the child stresses about his mistake, matched by The Temptations singing in unison the lines 'Listen to your heart beat/It's beating much too fast/Go back home where you belong'. It's an epic adventure for both the child and the group.

Like 'Cloud Nine', the instrumentation is dark and moody, reflecting the situation the child finds himself in. On the album version, there's plenty of room for the Funk Brothers to explore this new direction, with plenty of wah-wah guitar and organ, played by Earl Van Dyke. The vocals, as on 'Cloud Nine', are shared out among the group: Edwards takes the first verse, but the backing vocals are more complex than simply 'ooh's and 'ahh's, foreshadowing the rest of the song's message, and serving to act as the inner thoughts of the runaway child. All the members get a couple of lines to sing.

Released in early 1969 as a single, it was the third single release after 'Cloud Nine', sandwiched in between their take on the Christmas classics 'Rudolph The Red-Nosed Reindeer' backed with 'Silent Night', and the duet with Diana Ross & The Supremes, 'I'm Gonna Make You Love Me'. This time, this foray into psychedelia did one better than 'Cloud Nine' and topped the R&B charts and hit number six again on the pop charts. That version, though, was mixed down to a more suitable 4:53, which is still long by the group's earlier standards. Yet, it again proved to Whitfield that this was more than a passing fad, and set him up for the next major Temptations singles.

'Love Is A Hurtin' Thing' (Ben Raleigh, Dave Linden)
Side two of *Cloud Nine* returns the group to more familiar territory and features more filler material in the vein of their earlier albums. It begins with a cover of this Lou Rawls song, originally recorded in 1966, which gave Rawls both a pop and R&B hit, topping the latter. Franklin opens the first verse before Kendricks takes over, and then Edwards takes the lead for the second verse. None of them sound particularly like Rawls, but it's clear that Whitfield is very much into this new approach of splitting leads on a single song. It's certainly a pleasant cover, but it's just that – a decent album cut.

'Hey Girl' (Gerry Goffin, Carole King)
First recorded by Freddie Scott in 1963, this Goffin-King composition gave him an R&B and pop top-ten hit. Here, though, it's relegated to simply another pleasant piece of album filler. Paul Williams sings the entire lead, with the rest of The Temptations relegated back to singing 'ooh's and 'ahh's' throughout. Williams' lead, though, is particularly enjoyable, and he sounds even more emotional and plaintive than some of his earlier leads: by this time, he was having both financial and health problems, so perhaps they both fed into his vocal here. His vocal stops this version of 'Hey Girl' from being a run-of-the-mill cover, giving it a slight edge over some of the other B-side tracks on *Cloud Nine.*

'Why Did She Have To Leave Me (Why Did She Have To Go)' (Norman Whitfield, Barrett Strong)
More in keeping with their earlier collaborations than 'Cloud Nine' or 'Runaway Child, Running Wild', this is a typical Motown breakup song, on which Edwards plays the part of a heartbroken lover. Compared with his performance on the album's singles, Edwards is much more restrained here in his lead vocal – possibly still finding his feet as a Temptation, and maybe even trying to imitate the softer side of David Ruffin.

The backing vocals are straightforward, too, with plenty of 'ooh's and less creativity than other songs on the album, mirroring Edwards in the chorus, with Kendricks and Otis Williams prominent in the mix. Neither groundbreaking nor disappointing, 'Why Did She Have To Leave Me' is more pleasant album filler from Whitfield and Strong. It was also released as the B-side to the single release of 'Cloud Nine'.

'I Need Your Lovin'' (Norman Whitfield, Barrett Strong)
Released as the B-side to 'Runaway Child, Running Wild', 'I Need Your Lovin'' features a lead from Kendricks. Like Edwards on 'Why Did She Have To Leave Me', Kendricks sings somewhat more restrained than on his earlier singles, yet sounds as sweet as ever. The song itself is another generic love song with a Motown feel, not strong enough for a single release but perfectly fine to bulk out an album.

'Don't Let Him Take Your Love From Me' (Norman Whitfield, Barrett Strong)
Whitfield first recorded this song with Gladys Knight & The Pips in December 1967 and it was released as a single a month later. He clearly felt this song had more to offer, or rather, he had new ideas for the song, as not only did he record it for *Cloud Nine* with The Temptations, but he also tried it with Jimmy Ruffin, Four Tops and his pet project, The Undisputed Truth. Here, the lead is sung by Paul Williams, who gives a typically impassioned performance, sounding like he's singing while crying from heartbreak.

The instrumentation is pretty sparse, reflecting perhaps the story's song, although there is a big, brassy horn arrangement from the first chorus onwards. Like others on this side of *Cloud Nine*, it does feel like this is just another Motown-by-numbers album track, but Williams's lead performance saves it from becoming skippable.

'I Gotta Find A Way (To Get You Back)' (Norman Whitfield, Barrett Strong, Eddie Holland, Cornelius Grant, Eddie Kendricks)
A collaborative effort between Whitfield, Strong, Kendricks, Eddie Holland and Temptations guitarist and musical director Cornelius Grant, 'I Gotta Find A Way' sounds much more like an earlier Motown stomper than the group's new psychedelic sound. Indeed, it's not hard to imagine this being spun in

Britain's 'Northern Soul' clubs, with its pounding drum beat and bassline, sweetened by the swinging string arrangement. Edwards sings the lead, and, unlike 'Why Did She Have To Leave Me', shows no sign of restraint in his singing; instead, he shouts his way through the song, almost like a preacher, while the other Temptations do their best to keep up with his fast-paced delivery.

'Gonna Keep On Tryin' Til I Win Your Love' (Norman Whitfield, Barrett Strong)

Cloud Nine ends on another cover of an earlier Motown song by Whitfield and Strong. Edwin Starr first recorded 'Gonna Keep On Tryin' Til I Win Your Love' in 1967, and later, Jimmy Ruffin recorded a version before The Temptations had their turn. Later, Marvin Gaye and, unsurprisingly, The Undisputed Truth also recorded versions.

Edwards takes the lead on this version, although he is much softer in his approach than on 'I Gotta Find A Way', at times seeming to struggle to reach the higher notes in the song. Whitfield, it seems, applied his trademark technique of having an artist sing in a higher key than they're typically comfortable with, although this doesn't work as well as it did with David Ruffin or Marvin Gaye.

In fairness to Whitfield, though, he'd tried a more intense version with Starr, who shout-sings throughout his version, so it perhaps made sense to take a slightly different approach. Again, it's pleasant but nonetheless filler, and filler that required no further writing effort from Whitfield and Strong but ensured their publishing got another boost.

Puzzle People (1969)

Personnel:
Otis Williams, Melvin Franklin, Paul Williams, Eddie Kendricks, Dennis Edwards: vocals
The Funk Brothers: instrumentation
Produced at Hitsville USA, Detroit, by Norman Whitfield between October 1968 and July 1969
Label: Gordy
Release date: 23 September 1969
Length: 43:47
Charts: US Pop: 5, US R&B: 1, UK: 20

The success of *Cloud Nine* vindicated Whitfield's new sound to both Motown and The Temptations, and he continued with this new approach on *Puzzle People*, released just eight months after its predecessor. Whitfield continued his experimentation with longer tracks that take a more cinematic approach, featuring plenty of wah-wah guitars and moodier, darker arrangements. There would be far fewer ballads and a greater emphasis on message songs; on *Puzzle People*, Whitfield tackles race, money and power. The days of bright, up-tempo numbers and dreamy, romantic ballads were mostly over.

There are, of course, a few covers thrown in to pad the album out, including a cover of 'Hey Jude' by The Beatles. This was included, presumably, to placate Berry Gordy and the Motown leadership, with their traditional approach of not alienating a mainstream (white) audience, who might be put off listening to songs called 'Slave' or 'Message From A Black Man'. Whitfield clearly felt emboldened enough by his recent successes with the group to start writing such tracks, but didn't have the power, at least yet, to stop recording more mainstream covers. That would come shortly.

Unsurprisingly, then, it's the Whitfield-Strong collaborations that are the best on *Puzzle People*, with Whitfield continuing to draw inspiration from Sly & The Family Stone's pioneering sound, as well as James Brown's new brand of heavy-funk. This culminates on 'I Can't Get Next To You', a huge number-one hit on both the R&B and pop charts. On this, and on other tracks, Whitfield continued to share the verses between different members of the group, sharing leads on single songs. The songs also continue to get longer, with 'Message From A Black Man' hitting six minutes and 'Slave' reaching an unheard of – at least by Motown's standards – seven-and-a-half minutes long.

Interestingly, from a marketing perspective, *Puzzle People* was released on the same day that Motown also released *Together*, an album of duets with Diana Ross & The Supremes. *Together* was the second album to be released with both groups; the first, *Diana Ross & The Supremes Join The Temptations*, was released a year earlier, and both groups performed together in two television specials, *TCB* and *On Broadway*, with soundtrack albums from both also released. Both groups were at their peak, and Motown figured the public would buy any product that featured them both, resulting in *Together* (and the previous album), featuring mostly covers of Motown and other soul songs. Yet, thematically and sonically, the albums were very different: *Together* harked back to the group's past; *Puzzle People* hinted at their future.

Neither of the duet albums is as good as The Temptations' solo albums in this period, but there are some decent moments, including covers of 'I'm Gonna Make You Love Me' from the first album and 'Can't Take My Eyes Off You' from the second, featuring a rare lead from Mary Wilson. *Together* also features an ill-judged medley of 'My Guy, My Girl' in which Diana Ross and Dennis Edwards duet together somewhat awkwardly. The album also peaked at number five on the pop charts, but compared with *Puzzle People*, it's a less dynamic, less innovative and less rewarding listen.

'I Can't Get Next To You' (Norman Whitfield, Barrett Strong)
Released in July 1969 as the second single taken from *Puzzle People*, 'I Can't Get Next To You' is a love song disguised as a funk workout. Strong and Whitfield take a novel approach to the song's central love story: the narrator of the song is so powerful, so almighty, that he can 'make it rain', 'make a ship sail on dry land' and can even 'turn a grey sky blue'. Yet, the thing he really wants, the girl at the heart of the song, he cannot get. Therefore, as Edwards sings, his life is incomplete and he's blue.

Whitfield opens the song with the sound of an 'audience' clapping and shouting before Edwards interrupts, saying 'Hold it everybody, hold it, hold it, listen!'. As the 'audience' are immediately silenced, just Earl Van Dyke's piano is heard playing a short introduction before the song explodes and the other Funk Brothers, augmented by a brash horn arrangement, boom out. The Funk Brothers lay down a tight groove, with the chucking guitar dominant throughout, as is the percussion, with Eddie 'Bongo' Brown's playing prominent in the verses and Jack Ashford's tambourine in the choruses. This hard-hitting percussive beat allowed the group to devise some striking choreography, with Kendricks inventing a straight-legged dance move that the group still perform today.

The lead vocals are shared fairly evenly out: all five Temptations get a line to sing, while Edwards and Kendricks split the leads in the bridges and choruses.

Lyrically, it's a reversal of the Smokey Robinson-style lyrics of their earlier hits, which focus primarily on the beauty of the girl in question; here, no matter what the guy does, it's still not enough. This reaches a climax in the second bridge:

> 'Cause girl you're the key to my happiness
> And I
> Can't get next to you
> Girl, you're blowing my mind 'cause I can't get (next to you)

The strongest song on *Puzzle People* by far, 'I Can't Get Next To You' is rightly one of The Temptations' biggest hits and greatest songs; it was a double number-one hit on both the US pop and R&B charts in October 1969, and even reached number 13 on the UK singles chart. It again proved that this new lineup, led by the powerful Edwards, was worthy of The Temptations name. Otis Williams later recalled that 'when this hit, we started hearing 'David who?' Nothing against David, but our group had to keep keepin' on.'

The group also included versions on their live albums *Live At London's Talk Of The Town*, with what sounds like a huge horn section, and also on their *In Japan!* album, featuring replacement Temptations Richard Street and Damon Harris. Interestingly, no other Motown act covered the song; Whitfield didn't even record it on any of his other acts, like The Undisputed Truth. Presumably, this time, he felt he couldn't better his first attempt. However, plenty of other artists did cover the song, from the sublime Memphis soul of Al Green to the purely awful version recorded by The Osmonds.

'Hey Jude' (John Lennon, Paul McCartney)

The Beatles and Motown had a reciprocal admiration for each other: the lads from Liverpool admired the early 'Motown Sound' and famously covered some of the label's earliest hits, 'Please Mr Postman', 'You've Really Got A Hold On Me' and 'Money (That's What I Want)'. For his part, Gordy couldn't help but be impressed by their success and, from a purely business perspective, the group's covers had brought his company additional revenue. Motown also repaid the favour by having their acts record several Beatles covers; The Supremes' third album, *A Little Bit Of Liverpool*, saw the group cover a number of Lennon and McCartney songs (although it was panned by critics as pointless, and is somewhat of a challenging listen today).

In his autobiography, Otis Williams claimed that the group 'loved' recording 'Hey Jude', giving them an opportunity to record something not in the Jobete catalogue. Whitfield has the song open with electric guitar playing the song's melody before stripping out most of the instrumentation save for piano, and the group begin singing. Eventually, the musicians are all brought in again, while the lead is shared around the group, with everyone bar Otis Williams getting lines to sing. This approach, which worked well on 'I Can't Get Next To You', sounds disjointed here; given the beauty of the original version, the split lead here simply doesn't suit the song as well.

'Don't Let The Joneses Get You Down' (Norman Whitfield, Barrett Strong)

The first single from *Puzzle People*, another Whitfield-Strong message song, this time the duo deal with the age-old problem of keeping up with the neighbours, trying to outdo whatever it is they've done or bought. Strong writes of the dangers of living life this way, mainly the financial ramifications of spending money simply because of envy. Many at Motown could have heeded his warning.

Sonically, it borrows a lot from 'Runaway Child, Running Wild', with plenty of hi-hat on the drums, creating tension and urgency. The song opens with just piano and bass, followed by some guitar licks, then the hi-hat joins in along with the organ. Whitfield then strips the song back to just drums, bass and percussion before the first verse. Edwards sings the first verse with a fierce intensity, with Franklin chipping in a few words, while in the chorus, Kendricks is brought in to sweeten the sound, contrasting with Edwards, who is practically shouting his lyrics, and Franklin, who also mirrors Edwards' lyrics. Paul Williams is then given the first lines of the second verse before Kendricks takes it into the second chorus.

There's even a section that deals with the prospect of the Joneses buying a new car:

> Joneses got a new car today
> Here's what you should say
> (Hooray for the Joneses)
> Instead you worry 'til your whole head turns gray
> (Worryin' about the Joneses)
> Remember it's their car and they're the ones who had to pay
> So leave the Joneses alone
> Listen, your car might be old but, remember
> It never fails to get you where you want to go

The next section then discusses practical advice on how to save for something you want, rather than rushing into debt. This could be interpreted as Whitfield and Strong critiquing the growing consumerist culture in America, or simply sound financial advice. Either way, 'Don't Let The Joneses Get You Down' is another blistering stab of Motown-psychedlic-funk, perhaps overshadowed by 'I Can't Get Next To You', but thoroughly enjoyable thanks to the creative vocal arrangement and the rhythm and horn backing. An even more frantic version appeared on their *Live At Talk Of The Town London* album, released in 1970, backed by some impressive horn players.

'Message From A Black Man' (Norman Whitfield, Barrett Strong)
One of the more direct message songs Whitfield had The Temptations record, the lyrics by Strong would no doubt have given Gordy sleepless nights had the song been recorded a few years prior. Now, though, with a loyal audience and trust in Whitfield's new successful formula, risks like these could be taken. The lyrics certainly pulled no punches, immediately beginning with two lines, 'Yes, my skin is black/But that's no reason to hold me back'. The lyrics alternate between these more forceful lines and others where Whitfield and Strong promote equality between the races: after all, everyone has desires, black or white. The song ends by instructing the listener to 'look in the mirror'; we all have our faults, but the colour of your skin shouldn't determine your future.

The song foreshadows the direction Whitfield would take on 'Papa Was A Rolling Stone' in 1972; both are packed with wailing, fuzzy guitars, percussion, hi-hat drumming and a thumping bassline. The arrangement conveys a sense of urgency as the group repeat the line 'no matter how hard you try, you can't stop me now'. The lead is split between Kendricks, whose light falsetto contrasts with the solemn subject matter, and Edwards, who practically shouts his line. For most of the song, though, the group repeat that same line over and over, as Whitfield extends the song to six minutes.

For Motown, this was a huge statement, and it's certainly no surprise that this didn't feature on their duets album with The Supremes. Even Otis Williams, who was on board with Whitfield's creative direction, felt the song, and the album overall, was 'quite direct and maybe a little outspoken for some people's tastes.' However, perhaps because of the lyrics and their largely white audience, they never performed it live, though Williams claimed it did receive 'a lot of airplay'. Unusually for Whitfield, he didn't cut it on either the Undisputed Truth or Rare Earth, unlike other message songs first recorded by The Temptations (The Spinners recorded a version before they left Motown, however).

'It's Your Thing' (Ronald Isley, O'Kelly Isley, Rudolph Isley)
An intriguing choice of song to cover, 'It's Your Thing' was a major hit for The Isley Brothers after they left Motown. They signed with Motown in 1965 after having some success with their own T-Neck Records, but decided to throw their lot in with the growing Detroit label. Yet, their time at Motown was an unhappy one: despite the vocal abilities of Ronald Isley and the trio's writing ability, they felt they were second-tier acts compared to The Temptations, Four Tops and Supremes. The group did have two big UK singles, 'Behind A Painted Smile' and 'This Old Heart Of Mine', but this wasn't enough, and they left the label in 1968. In 1969, they scored a major hit with 'It's Your Thing', a roaring slab of funk that was somewhat of a rebuke to the more standard fare they had recorded at Motown.

Perhaps Whitfield was goading Gordy when he had The Temptations record it for *Puzzle People*. After The Isley Brothers had a huge hit with it, he took them to court, claiming they'd recorded the song while under contract to Motown. A judge eventually found in The Isleys' favour.

It's unlikely The Isleys would have lost any sleep over this version as it's far less funky and infectious than their original; instead, it's given a Motown gloss that doesn't really work. Edwards sings the lead, which Whitfield then drenches in echo and surrounds with fuzzy guitars, which lack the crispness or funk of the original. As covers go, this is not one to return to.

'Little Green Apples' (Bobby Russell)
Another interesting choice of cover, 'Little Green Apples' was written by Bobby Russell and was initially a hit for country artist Roger Miller before

Patti Page and soul singer O.C. Smith released their own hit versions. Equally interesting, Four Tops also recorded a version for their 1969 album *Four Tops Now!*

The lead is given to Paul Williams, who gives it his trademark sorrowful edge, his vocal both haunting and beautiful, sounding like a man singing through his mental anguish. Whitfield keeps the production fairly sparse, sounding not unlike a Jimmy Webb number, leaving plenty of room for Williams to sing and wail. Indeed, it's essentially a Paul Williams solo song; the other Temptations aren't anywhere to be found – there's no backing vocals at all. Yet, it's one of the highlights of *Puzzle People*, purely for his vocal.

'You Don't Love Me No More' (Norman Whitfield, Barrett Strong, Roger Penzabene)

Written before Penzabene's death and dusted off for *Puzzle People,* as with 'I Wish It Would Rain', it, too, drew on the breakdown of his marriage, still unable to come to terms with her alleged affair. Unlike Penzabene's previous recordings with the group, this is a more up-tempo affair, almost danceable, as Kendricks takes the lead, singing about another man taking his place in the relationship. It's almost as if Kendricks is pleased with the outcome, though he doesn't outright declare that to the girl in the story. Had Penzabene been alive, or maybe even with Edwards or Paul Williams on lead, the song might have mirrored those on *Wish It Would Rain*, reflecting more accurately the intense pain he felt over the breakup of his marriage.

'Since I've Lost You' (Norman Whitfield)

First recorded by Jimmy Ruffin in 1964, Whitfield had already revisited the song once with Gladys Knight & The Pips in 1967. After all, why bother writing something new to fill out *Puzzle People*, and, as filler tracks go, 'Since I've Lost You' is a pretty song that has Edwards on lead, singing to his former lover about how she's left him so blue. The backing harmonies hark back to their more doo-wop influenced early singles, while Whitfield keeps the arrangement and production mellow, with the string section mixed fairly until the bridge, where Franklin delivers a couple of spoken-word lines.

'Running Away (Ain't Gonna Help You)' (Norman Whitfield, Barrett Strong)

Released as the B-side to 'I Can't Get Next To You', 'Running Away' again returns the group to more standard soul fare. It's a pleading ballad with Paul Williams on lead, who plays the part of a man who simply won't give up on his woman, even if she's literally running away. It's romantic, with Williams singing the lyrics with enough conviction and raw emotion to sound like a broken man rather than simply a stalker.

The track opens with Eddie 'Bongo' Brown playing his bongos before two duelling guitars join in and, eventually, the drums and bass drop in, too. There are no strings or horns, but plenty of backing harmonies, with Kendricks prominent on the highs, serving as a counterweight to Williams' despairing, soulful lead. And given his own personal problems, Williams probably didn't need to dig too deep to tap into this emotion.

'That's The Way Love Is' (Norman Whitfield, Barrett Strong)
First recorded by The Isley Brothers and released in 1967, it was then covered in 1969 by Marvin Gaye, becoming a number-seven US pop hit for Gaye when it was released as a single in August. It would likely have topped the R&B chart, too, but was held off by none other than The Temptations with 'I Can't Get Next To You'.

On *Puzzle People*, though, it's relegated to album filler, although Whitfield doesn't skimp on the production. It's given a psychedelic makeover, with a vocal arrangement that could have been stolen from Sly & The Family Stone. Edwards sings the bulk of the lead, shouting his way through the song, although Paul Williams contributes a verse. Whitfield layers plenty of percussion and guitar on the track, mixing the bass high, too. The tempo changes in the choruses, giving it a slight jazz feel. It's another strong album cut, once again showing how Whitfield could reinterpret his own songs depending on who he was producing.

'Slave' (Norman Whitfield, Barrett Strong)
Puzzle People ends with a seven-minute-long psychedelic-funk odyssey, telling the story of slavery from the perspective of a slave. Edwards and Kendricks share the lead vocals, and both deliver impassioned performances, with Edwards basically shouting his lines.

Lyrically, Strong pulls no punches about the brutal treatment of slaves, the first verse setting the depressing scene for the rest of the song, in which the slave realises this is how he'll spend his life:

> In the morning I slave in the hot sun for little or no wage
> At night I'm locked in, like an animal in a cage
> Man stunted on me with a gun
> Sayin' 'I bet a man'
> Oh, in a hole I have to spend
> The rest of my time

'Slave' foreshadows the longer songs Whitifield would include on future Temptations records, particularly those from the album *Solid Rock* onwards, once Kendricks and Paul Williams had left the group. On 'Slave', The Temptations only provide vocals for the first half of the song; the rest is largely instrumental, dominated by the guitars, either playing licks or making liberal use of the wah-wah pedal.

The Temptations do return just as the song comes to an end, singing the line 'Free me from this ball and chain, somebody/Somebody help this slave' repeatedly. Gordy's mantra of 'Keep It Simple, Stupid' and his aversion to political songs were now clearly a thing of the past.

Psychedelic Shack (1970)

Personnel:
Otis Williams, Melvin Franklin, Paul Williams, Eddie Kendricks, Dennis Edwards: vocals
The Funk Brothers: instrumentation
Produced at Hitsville USA, Detroit, by Norman Whitfield between November 1969 and February 1970
Label: Gordy
Release date: 6 March 1970
Length: 36:37
Charts: US Pop: 9, US R&B: 1

Despite the success of the new 'psychedelic soul' on both *Cloud Nine* and *Puzzle People*, The Temptations were beginning to show signs of a split over this new sound. Kendricks, in particular, was never keen on this new direction and had quickly grown tired of singing these 'message songs'. He favoured a return to their more traditional material, with the emphasis put back on love rather than social issues. Kendricks later told Sharon Davis:

> I must admit that I don't dig those weird, freaky sounds; they're not my type of thing. The direction the group is going in is not for me. I like the old sounds we used to record, sounds that have good melodies, and I wish we'd do some stuff like that again.

In fairness to Whitfield, his productions with The Temptations, compared with Sly & The Family Stone's then-current releases, were much more tame, and Whitfield wasn't about to return to the past. Kendricks would have to wait for his wish to come true, as *Psychedelic Shack* largely picks up where *Puzzle People* left off, with Whitfield forging ahead with his brand of experimental soul. Even the album cover is more experimental, placing the group in a multicoloured shack wearing some funky threads. The days of The Temptations looking smart in fancy suits on their album covers were over.

Psychedelic Shack is also the group's first album to feature only compositions written by Whitfield and Strong; there's no material from other Motown writers, and no non-Motown covers. Given the impressive sales and hits Whitfield was producing for the group, Motown were content to let him get on with the job, with the added bonus of boosting the royalties for Whitfield and Strong.

Overall, *Psychedelic Shack* is a strong, intense album, with plenty of excellent vocal performances from The Temptations backed by increasingly complex arrangements and new sounds. Whitfield uses reverb, echo, tape effects and stereo panning, combined with sound effects of doors opening, background chattering and other noises to fully immerse the listener in the 'shack' as an actual place. He also embraces the 'psychedelic soul' developed by Sly Stone, making heavy use of guitars which are fuzzed and distorted, more common in rock and funk music than Motown's brand of soul.

The softer moments are few and far between here; instead, Whitfield and Strong use the album to tell a story about the brutal human experience, from poverty, religion and, of course, war. It's certainly miles away from *In A Mellow Mood* or *With A Lot O' Soul*, but Whitfield was both determined and convinced his ideas would work, even if that meant alienating the very people he was recording.

'Psychedelic Shack' (Norman Whitfield, Barrett Strong)

The album opens with the same introduction Whitfield used on 'I Can't Get Next To You', but this time, Whitfield adds the sound of a creaking door, which opens to reveal an audience, presumably in a shack, clapping and hollering, with Edwards urging them to listen. Then, out blasts a loud wail on the guitar, and the Funk Brothers launch into one of the funkiest grooves The Temptations had the pleasure to sing over.

Strong's lyrics depict a nightclub frequented by counter-culture types, where 'to get in it don't take much dough', but once inside, 'you can really do your thing', whether that's dancing or taking 'a look at your mind' – in other words, taking drugs. Everyone goes to the psychedelic shack, from kings and queens to poets to hippies. It's an imagined paradise of racial and class equality, where everyone can 'join in and be what you want to be'.

The Funk Brothers lay down a monstrous groove, aided by late addition to the band Dennis Coffey on guitar, whose wah-wah effects open up the track. Whitfield uses the full breadth of the stereo track to cram in as much as possible: wah-wah guitars, loud drums and percussion, a pulsating bassline and, of course, the vocals. The lead, like most of their psychedelic soul tracks, is split: Edwards takes the bulk, but Kendricks and Paul Williams get plenty of moments, too; even Otis Williams gets a couple of lines.

Franklin trades with Kendricks on the line, 'So high you can't get over it/ So love you can't get under it', matching their falsetto and bass, respectively. This line, or versions of it, appears in gospel numbers and other R&B and funk songs. It tells the listener that God's love is so great that it cannot be avoided; the only way 'in' is through the 'door', which can be understood as Christ, salvation or the church (George Clinton used a similar phrase on Funkadelic's epic 'One Nation Under A Groove'). Here then, entering the 'psychedelic shack' could be a metaphor for salvation.

Released just after Christmas in 1969, backed with 'That's The Way Love Is', it reached number two and seven on the R&B and pop charts, respectively, although it could only reach number 33 on the UK singles chart. The single version clocks in at a radio-friendly 3:48; Whitfield produced an extended six-minute version, but, sadly, this blisteringly funky version was only finally issued on the 2003 compilation *Psychedelic Soul*.

'You Make Your Own Heaven And Hell Right Here On Earth' (Norman Whitfield, Barrett Strong)

The closest The Temptations ever got to being fire-and-brimstone preachers, this is essentially a short sermon that deals with the issue of free will. Strong's lyrics play on the Christian influence that The Temptations and their fans had, reminding the listener that it's their decisions in life that determine how they'll spend eternity, so they'd better start considering their actions.

The song begins with some heavenly-sounding strings as the group sing 'Kumba-ya-ya', drawing on the religious standard 'Kumbaya, My Lord'. All The Temptations, bar Paul Williams, share lead vocal duties, although naturally, given the song's ferocity, Edwards dominates the performance. The Funk Brothers once again impress on this new sound, changing tempo with ease, and building tension in the chorus by upping the pace. A truly great album track, it ended up as the B-side to the single release of the ballad 'Just My Imagination (Running Away With Me)' a year later. Whitfield's other band, The Undisputed Truth, also recorded a version the year after.

'Hum Along And Dance' (Norman Whitfield, Barrett Strong)

This is essentially an instrumental song with Edwards, Kendricks and Franklin switching between singing the chorus, if you can call it that, as well as scatting and vocalising. The only lyrics explain the song's premise: 'Ain't no words to this song, you just dance and hum along'.

Given the short length of the previous song, somehow Whitfield manages to extend the song out to nearly four minutes, featuring a pounding rhythm track, padded out by plenty of guitar effects and panning. It's certainly a funk jam, and hints at the direction Whitfield took on future tracks, making the most of longer instrumental breaks and less input from the group.

Towards the end, the group sing in unison, shouting like fans at a sports match, 'Come on man, take a drag, don't be afraid, it ain't gonna hurt you' – a reference to marijuana use. The song then segues into the next track. Once the drugs take effect, we can take a trip through our minds.

The song was later recorded by Rare Earth, whose version is far more rock-oriented, and, oddly, given their clean-cut all-American image, The Jackson 5 also recorded a cover for their *G.I.T. Get It Together* album in 1973.

'Take A Stroll Thru Your Mind' (Norman Whitfield, Barrett Strong)

After we've accepted the kind offer of drag on the group's weed, Whitfield slows the pace down and we're invited to take a stroll through our own mind. Kendricks opens the song, singing 'One drag is all it took, I'm hooked', and that 'you'll be surprised what you might find' if you partake. Whitfield pares back the instrumentation, so it's largely just bongos and bass. He also doubles the lead vocals from Kendricks and Edwards, so they're singing with themselves, a technique Marvin Gaye would master on *What's Going On*.

Whitfield stretches the song to nearly eight minutes, sounding a little repetitive at times, although the atmosphere changes around the three-and-a-half-minute mark with a rock-style guitar solo, more suited to the Funkadelic records than The Temptations'. The rest of the group are eventually given lines to sing, with Paul Williams taking the lead in the third verse, singing a further verse about how rough his week is until Friday comes around and the drugs come out, when 'the eagle flies, huh, and so do I'. There's then a blues guitar solo as Kendricks finishes the song once more with the chorus, then another rock-sounding guitar solo before Whitfield strips the song back to the bongos and bass, as Kendricks invites us once more to get high.

'It's Summer' (Norman Whitfield, Barrett Strong)
After the opening four numbers, Whitfield returns to more familiar territory with the ballad 'It's Summer', featuring Franklin who speaks all the song's verses rather than singing, telling us all about the beauties of the 'happiest season of them all'. The rest of The Temptations back him with some suitably sweet harmonies, singing that there's 'magic in the air, green grass everywhere'. It's a marked contrast to the previous songs. Perhaps we're still high from the fumes in the psychedelic shack, but it does break up the album's intensity. The group later re-recorded the song for the *Solid Rock* album, their first without both Paul Williams and Eddie Kendricks. This re-recorded version was also released as a single.

'War' (Barrett Strong, Norman Whitfield)
Before Whitfield produced Edwin Starr's classic version of 'War', he first tried it out on The Temptations. At the time Strong and Whitfield were writing the song, America was still fighting in Vietnam, with no end in sight, and the Nixon administration would soon escalate the conflict with the bombing of Cambodia. It was also a war in which African-American conscripts were more likely to be injured or killed.

Strong had personally been affected by the war: one of his cousins had been badly wounded in Vietnam, while one of his friends had returned with life-changing injuries. He could no longer stay silent about the situation in his music.

Yet, considering the lyrics, it's surprising that Whitfield recorded the song with the group at all: could the notoriously politically cautious Motown risk their top male act being seen as anti-war and therefore unpatriotic? As their version wasn't released as a single, Motown simply hedged its bets. Yet, it also more likely reflects the fact that this version simply isn't very good.

Whereas Starr's version blasts out of the speaker, taking no hostages, exploding like a barrage of artillery against Viet Cong, The Temptations' version is a much cheesier affair. The arrangement itself lacks any punch, not helped by Whitfield having Franklin repeat 'Hup-two-three-four, hup-two-three-four' over and over, as if he were a drill sergeant on the parade ground.

It doesn't strike the right tone, and Whitfield smartly didn't repeat it on Starr's version. Here, the lead vocals are split between Paul Williams and Edwards, whose vocals are always impeccable, but they lack the punch that Starr was able to deliver later on. Whitfield's production is careful not to appear too brash or bold, and as a result, Strong's lyrics fail to cut through.

There was, of course, less risk in recording the song with Edwin Starr. Motown clearly had no such qualms about Starr re-recording the song in a brasher, harsher way, though; Starr had only minor hits up until 'War', and it was his version of the song that he became synonymous with throughout the rest of his career.

'You Need Love Like I Do (Don't You)' (Norman Whitfield, Barrett Strong)
Possibly the only song on the album that could be labelled a love song, 'You Need Love Like I Do (Don't You)' is a funk workout in which doo-wop influenced vocals meet the intense Whitfield sound. Kendricks sings a beautiful lead, although this is contrasted somewhat by the intense pace and instrumentation of the song. Whitfield throws lots into the mix here: naturally, there's plenty of guitar, along with a creative horn arrangement and a healthy dose of percussion and tambourine. As a result, Kendricks' lead is overshadowed by the instrumentation. Edwards might have been able to dominate a track like this, but Kendricks, longing for the softer ballads, struggles to keep up.

'Friendship Train' (Norman Whitfield, Barrett Strong)
First recorded by Gladys Knight & The Pips in 1969, a hit single for the quartet, Whitfield once again recycled one of his efforts for The Temptations. Unfortunately, not much effort went into reimagining the track for the group; the arrangements are almost identical, except for the fact that the version here is almost double in length, stretching to nearly eight minutes. Edwards takes the lead and introduces the song like Sly Stone did on 'Dance To The Music', counting off musicians. The backing vocals are mixed lower, making the song essentially a vehicle for Edwards to growl and shout from. The guitars are front and centre, and the horns blaze through a deep, brash arrangement. It's a fitting end to *Psychedelic Shack*, Whitfield's most ambitious effort with the group yet.

'Ball Of Confusion (That's What The World Is Today)' (Norman Whitfield, Barrett Strong)
The pinnacle of The Temptations' message songs, and one of their biggest-selling, 'Ball Of Confusion' wasn't included on any of their albums. Instead, it was first released as a single in May 1970, recorded just a few weeks before its release, and appeared on their *Greatest Hits II* collection, which brought together their biggest-selling 'psychedelic soul' hits. It reached number three

and number two on the pop and R&B charts, respectively.

The song begins with a count-off before the bass falls in, joined after a few bars by plenty of wah-wah guitar played by Dennis Coffey. Whitfield creates a dark cinematic soundscape, reflecting Strong's lyrics and the fast-paced delivery of them by the group. The lead is split between all Temptations (except Otis Williams), with Kendricks and Edwards sharing the first verse and Paul Williams and Edwards the second. The lyrics pull no punches from the start, with Kendricks singing 'People movin' out, people movin' in/Why? Because the colour of their skin'. It sets the tone for the rest of the song, and it's all here: drugs, segregation, war, politics, violence. Edwards' delivery is phenomenal, somehow managing to enunciate the words 'segregation, determination, demonstration, integration, aggravation, humiliation, obligation to our nation' at breakneck speed.

Strong's lyrics reflect an America gone wrong after the promise of the early 1960s: he references The Beatles, hippie culture, lamenting that all of that is gone, replaced instead by war and violence. Edwards screams out in desperation, 'Great Googa Mooga, can't you hear me talking to you!', demanding the audience take heed to the song's message – but the song doesn't offer any solutions. After all, the world carries on; as Franklin sings several times, 'the band played on'.

It struck a nerve with their audience, giving the group another hit on both the R&B and pop charts, hitting number two and number three, respectively, and even broke the top ten in the UK Singles Chart.

Unsurprisingly, Whitfield also recorded it with the Undisputed Truth and released it on their self-titled debut album; their version features an almost identical backing track, extended to over ten minutes in length. Edin Starr also recorded a version for his *Revolver* album. The most famous cover, though, is Tina Turner's 1982 version, which was the first step on her magnificent comeback.

Sky's The Limit (1971)

Personnel:
Otis Williams, Melvin Franklin, Paul Williams, Eddie Kendricks, Dennis Edwards: vocals
The Funk Brothers: instrumentation
David Van De Pitte: arrangements
Jerry Long: arrangement on 'Just My Imagination (Running Away With Me)'
Produced at Hitsville USA, Detroit, by Norman Whitfield between August 1970 and March 1971
Mastering: Norman Whitfield, Orsen Lewis
Label: Gordy
Release date: 22 April 1971
Length: 43:26
Charts: US Pop: 16, US R&B: 2

Sky's The Limit marked the closing of another chapter in The Temptations' saga: by the time the album was released, both Eddie Kendricks and Paul Williams had left the group, leaving Otis Williams and Melvin Franklin, neither of whom would be considered 'lead singers', as the last two original members. This was no surprise to either man, however.

Kendricks had grown further away from the group as time had gone on; always a bit of a loner, he appeared more isolated since Ruffin left in 1968, and didn't fully embrace the more experimental sounds and messages that Whitfield was recording with the group. He had also begun expressing his desire for a solo record, but remained with the group even if he was increasingly uneasy with the message songs Whitfield had forced upon them. One night, after a performance at the Westbury Music Fair, Kendricks and Franklin began arguing, almost coming to blows. Otis Williams recalled in his autobiography that the 'fighting always upset me because you never could predict where it was going to end.' That night, after tempers had cooled, he and Franklin went for a walk, discussing the group's future. He later wrote:

> We promised each other we'd keep going no matter what, even if we had to do it without Eddie or Paul. Don't misunderstand: we didn't want to lose them, but we felt very strongly that things were moving in that direction.

Then, during an engagement at the Copacabana in New York, Otis Williams' mother passed away. Heartbroken, Williams returned home to his family briefly before rejoining The Temptations in New York to finish their scheduled dates. During one performance, according to him, after he hit a bum note, Kendricks shot him a look of disgust. Fearing a confrontation offstage, Williams moved dressing rooms with Franklin joining him, but this only inflamed Kendricks more. Kendricks didn't show for the rest of the engagement, and it was then that the rest of the group decided to kick Kendricks out.

He officially left the group in March 1971, and despite his later claims about mismanagement of his and the group's career and finances at Motown, he remained with the label and had a decent solo career, with R&B hits like 'Keep on Truckin'', 'Boogie Down' and 'Girl (Can I Have A Change Of Mind)' becoming an important influence on the emerging disco scene. He could never escape his past as a Temptation, however, and in 1982, along with Ruffin, rejoined the group for a tour and an album. When that ended, he and Ruffin, and later Dennis Edwards, went on the road, hitting the oldies circuit playing The Temptations' greatest hits.

In Paul Williams' case, his departure was not his choice. His health was failing (he was diagnosed with sickle cell disease), not helped by his increased alcohol intake. The group already hired Richard Street to sing his parts offstage, allowing Williams to save his voice for his solo numbers. But that was simply an interim solution to a larger dilemma, and eventually, it became clear that he couldn't carry on performing. Otis Williams later couldn't recall Paul's last performance with the group, but no-one wanted to be the one to tell him, 'our soul, our creative leader', that he would have to stop performing. Luckily for them, when Paul finally saw a doctor, he did the job for them: he told him he could no longer perform in his current state. He was kept on the payroll and acted as a consultant of sorts, but his days as a Temptation were over.

As a result, some of the tracks on the album do not feature Kendricks, recorded just after he left but before a replacement was officially brought in. *Sky's The Limit* continues in a similar vein to *Psychedelic Shack*, although Whitfield includes more ballads on this album as opposed to the message and social commentary songs he had recently favoured. Indeed, the album's standout track is the ballad 'Just My Imagination', somewhat of a throwback to their earlier love songs and very much against the direction of travel Whitfield was taking the group. With its gorgeous melody and equally beautiful lead vocals from Kendricks, it sold over a million copies as a single and served as Kendricks' swan song – a fitting way to bow out of the group. However, this proved to be a temporary reprieve, as the group's next album, *Solid Rock*, took a darker and depressing turn.

'Gonna Keep On Tryin' Til I Win Your Love' (Norman Whitfield, Barrett Strong)

Not content with recording the song for the *Cloud Nine* album, Whitfield revisited it once again for *Sky's The Limit*, producing a much more stripped-back version with Kendricks rather than Edwards on lead vocals. It sets the scene for what's to come on the rest of the album, though it does smack somewhat of scraping the barrel marked 'material', given the group had already recorded it.

The instrumentation is sparse: the first verse is mostly just Kendricks accompanied by guitar; it's not until the second verse that the strings, drums, bass and percussion fall in. With Kendricks' sweet falsetto, this version is much more relaxed and romantic than the earlier version, where Edwards shouts his way through the lyrics. It's pleasant but forgettable, and it's eclipsed by the rest of the album.

'Just My Imagination (Running Away With Me)' (Norman Whitfield, Barrett Strong)

Given the group's increasing complaints that Whitfield was focusing too much on message and political songs, he and Strong could still produce these incredible ballads when called for. Indeed, 'Just My Imagination' must surely rank as one of Whitfield and Strong's finest collaborations, gifting The Temptations one of their signature tunes and allowing Kendricks to exit the group on a high.

Although it's suitably soft and romantic, like so many Motown songs, the lyrics tell a somewhat darker, more depressing story. Kendricks plays the part of a man who allows his imagination to run away with itself, pretending he has a perfect life with the woman he desires. However, he realises, in the choruses, that this is nothing more than an illusion, a self-deception, recognising finally that, at the end of the song, 'in reality, she doesn't even know me'.

Whitfield keeps the instrumentation pretty sparse, creating an almost dream-like feel, reflecting the daydreaming of the song's narrator, as he lets his mind wander and construct this idyllic life. The group loved the initial track, hearing it without the strings, recognising the beauty of the song, and appreciating the fact that it was a welcome return to recording a ballad.

The string and horn arrangement by Jerry Long is equally subtle, contributing to the song's dreamy feel but also reflecting the melancholy at the core of the song. The strings are mixed low in the verse before the French horns combine in the bridge. It begins to soar at the moment when Paul Williams delivers, 'every night on my knees I pray'. Knowing these two men would soon be out of the group gives 'Just My Imagination' an extra poignancy when listening after the fact, allowing the two founding members to exit on an artistic and commercial triumph.

The vocals were recorded at Motown's Hitsville studios in Detroit on a cold December night in 1970, with Whitfield taking hours to record just the backing vocals before forcing Kendricks to endure even more to get the perfect lead vocal. Williams recalled being knocked out by Kendricks' performance, even though relations between them were frosty at best. He later wrote, 'I called him the next day to let him know I was concerned about how hard he worked and appreciated his efforts.' But their relationship couldn't be repaired, even if Williams later called the song 'Eddie's finest moment.'

The song became a pop and R&B number-one smash in the spring of 1971, and even hit the UK Singles Chart at a highly impressive number eight. Yet, the success was bittersweet with the departure of Kendricks and

Paul Williams just a few months later, leaving new members to perform the song in concert. Before they left, the group lip-synched to a version on *The Ed Sullivan Show* live in January 1971. The group were staged somewhat prophetically, with Kendricks sitting apart from the group in the foreground, with the others in the background. The group should have been enjoying their latest success, but the performance shows a group looking miserable and depressed, making it clear to anyone watching that this lineup wouldn't last much longer.

'I'm The Exception To The Rule' (Norman Whitfield, Barrett Strong)
The sad ballads continue with another sparse affair, the slightly depressing 'I'm The Exception To The Rule', a shared lead between Kendricks and Edwards, which ended up as the B-side to the single release of 'It's Summer'.

The song begins with an opening monologue from Williams, something that he would consider his 'niche' on later recordings. Kendricks sings the first lead lines before Edwards, at his shouty best, takes over; at times, it's clear the engineer was struggling to capture a clean take from Edwards as the track peaks and distorts under the sheer power of his vocal. The two swap around again on lead as the song comes to a conclusion. Paul Williams and Franklin, though, don't seem to be on the song as there is no discernible backing vocals. Instead, it's just Kendricks, Edwards and a dramatic string arrangement put together by David Van De Pitte.

'Smiling Faces Sometimes' (Norman Whitfield, Barrett Strong)
A 12-and-a-half-minute odyssey, 'Smiling Faces Sometimes' foreshadows the longer experimental tracks that Whitfield would master on the albums *All Directions*, *Masterpiece* and *1990*. The Temptations' version was the original to be recorded, although Whitfield re-recorded it with The Undisputed Truth later in 1971, and their version was released as a single and became a major pop hit. Here, though, with Kendricks on lead, any hope of it being released as a single was dashed when he left the group before it could be released; an edited version was ready to be issued, but instead, Whitfield went and recut 'It's Summer' with the four remaining Temptations, which was later included on the *Solid Rock* album.

Although Kendricks sings the bulk of the lead, Edwards sings the bridge and further lines in the song, while the backing harmonies are largely simple and repeat the title. On this long version, though, the focus is less on The Temptations' vocals and more on the cinematic arrangement. Here, it's clear he was experimenting with longer instrumental breakdowns and reducing the group's vocal input, again something that would become more common on future records.

That said, it's a phenomenal track: Whitfield creates an eerie, almost haunted feel, with a dramatic string arrangement interacting with plenty of wah-wah guitars, interspersed with a big brass section. The lyrics contain a message to the listener: beware of the smiling faces and the friendly pats on the back, as they 'don't tell the truth'. It's a message several of The Temptations could have heeded, too, when dealing with groupies and the hangers-on. It could also possibly be interpreted as a not-so-subtle dig at Ruffin and Kendricks from Whitfield and Strong.

'Man' (Norman Whitfield, Barrett Strong)
From the incredible lengths of 'Smiling Faces Sometimes', Whitfield then recorded 'Man', a short song featuring another message, this time warning about the upcoming destruction of man at his own hand. Strong's lyrics are certainly depressing, made more so by the sparse instrumentation: there's a beat played throughout that sounds like someone hammering away on a piece of wood, reflecting perhaps a 'man at work', upon which there's some light piano playing and a string arrangement. The hammering, though, is quite irritating, making repeated listens painful.

The lyrics are concise; Whitfield and Strong are trying to send the message that, yes, man has conquered everything, even the moon, but he won't and can't stop fighting his fellow man and won't stop searching for answers, which they find 'really kinda sad'. For them, this desire to conquer all is driving man away from God, away from his fellow man and friends, to a life of loneliness and eventually 'the end'. Not one of the most cheerful Temptations songs, but certainly their most existentialist.

'Throw A Farewell Kiss' (Norman Whitfield, Barrett Strong)
An early Whitfield-Strong collaboration, 'Throw A Farewell Kiss' was first recorded by Freddie Gorman in the early 1960s, although his version remained unheard in the Motown vault until its release in 2012. Gorman's biggest success at Motown came from co-writing for The Marvelettes, but The Velvelettes also released a version of 'Throw A Farewell Kiss' in 1964, recorded in a more traditional Motown style than the version on *Sky's The Limit*.

Edwards sings a restrained lead on this new version, backed by just piano, drums and distorted guitar. The other Temptations provide plenty of backing vocals, a combination of 'ooh's and echoes of the lyrics. The song features another relationship ending, with the narrator graciously setting free his girl if there's another she loves, throwing her a farewell kiss as she departs. Given the story, Edwards doesn't break out into his trademark shout; rather, he plays the part of a subdued, broken man.

The song seems to borrow a line from William Bell's debut single 'You Don't Miss Your Water' on Stax Records, as Edwards tells his girl if her new love should also falter, 'But listen, you won't miss your water until your well runs dry'.

'Throw A Farewell Kiss' is unlikely to make many Temptations 'Greatest Hits' collections, but it's undoubtedly another forgotten gem.

'Ungena Za Ulimwengu (Unite The World)' (Norman Whitfield, Barrett Strong)

After the mellow sounds of the previous track, Whitfield jolts the listener out of any casual listening with 'Ungena Za Ulimwengu', which is a Swahili phrase that translates in English as 'Unite The World'. The song begins with a loud combination of rock guitars, harmonica and blazing horns before the track settles into the first verse.

Another message song, 'Ungena Za Ulimwengu' is both pessimistic and optimistic: recorded in the context of the Nixon administration, the Vietnam War and the Cold War, Whitfield and Strong claim that peace, not love, is the greatest force in the world, and that it's the job of everyone to overcome the forces of division in society to achieve this. The lyrics certainly cover a lot of ground, from wiretapping to war to kidnapping to race relations. Franklin even asks in the first verse, 'Will the Russians push the button?'

After setting the scene, Whitfield and Strong then switch to more optimistic lyrics, although interestingly, they include a powerful message on race. Berry Gordy had largely prevented his acts from making such statements as he felt Motown's music should appeal to all, but here he must have relented. Still, it would be hard to disagree with the song's message, summed up in the following lines:

> This unrest between races has got to come to an end
> Don't let the color of my skin confuse you

Edwards sings the bulk of the lead, unrestrained this time, sounding simultaneously passionate and exasperated as the song reaches its climax. It's a phenomenal lead performance, not dissimilar to his vocals on 'Ball Of Confusion', where he approaches the song almost like a preacher, often shouting the lyrics with intense grit.

Released as a single in September 1970, it peaked at a middling number 33 on the pop charts but broke the top ten on the R&B charts. With its more political and rock edge, it's no surprise this wasn't a major pop hit with mainstream, whiter audiences. Predictably, Whitfield later revisited the song and recorded it on The Undisputed Truth's second album, combining it with 'Friendship Train' – which both The Temptations and Gladys Knight & The Pips previously recorded – to make a medley.

'Love Can Be Anything (Can't Nothing Be Love But Love)' (Norman Whitfield, Barrett Strong)

Sky's The Limit ends with another intense, pulsating song on which Edwards and Kendricks share the lead vocals. It opens with electric piano and distorted guitar before the horn arrangement kicks in, with the horns wailing throughout the song, particularly in the choruses and in the breakdowns. There's plenty of percussion, too, especially from Funk Brother Jack Ashford, the famed tambourine player, who goes all out.

The song itself is something of a message song about the importance of love and how 'love can be anything'; it perhaps made more sense to Whitfield and Strong in their era, but comes across as naive and idealistic today. Lyrics aside, the instrumentation from the Funk Brothers and the arrangement by David Van De Pitte are both excellent. The length of the song, however, lets it down: Whitfield drags it out for nearly eight minutes, throwing in plenty of guitar solos and horns while The Temptations are reduced to simply singing the song's title repeatedly. Was this a Temptations song, or a Whitfield track where The Temptations were simply contracted to provide some backing vocals?

Solid Rock (1972)

Personnel:
Otis Williams, Melvin Franklin, Dennis Edwards, Richard Street, Damon Harris, Paul Williams: vocals
Dennis Coffey, Eddie Willis, Joe Messina, Robert White, Melvin 'Wah Wah' Ragin: guitar
Richard 'Pistol' Allen, Andrew Smith, Aaron Smith: drums
Earl Van Dyke: piano
Johnny Griffith: organ
Leroy Taylor, James Jamerson: bass
Jack Ashford: tambourine, maracas, sticks
Jack Brokensha: timpani, vibes, bells, gourd
Eddie 'Bongo' Brown: bongo, congo
Paul Riser, David Van DePitte: arrangements
Produced at Hitsville USA, Detroit, by Norman Whitfield between May 1971 and January 1972
Mastering engineers: Norman Whitfield, Orson Lewis
Label: Gordy
Release date: 11 January 1972
Length: 38:48
Charts: US pop: 24, US R&B: 1, UK: 34

'Never before in the history of the record business has a group faced as many internal problems and been able to overcome them as The Temptations', wrote Norman Whitfield in the liner notes to *Solid Rock*. Indeed, the album heralded the arrival of two new Temptations and was the first album to be recorded without Paul Williams and Eddie Kendricks. Less than ten years since their first recordings, Otis Williams and Melvin Franklin were the only original members remaining, and neither sang much lead. Important as they were, new members were needed to fill their depleted ranks. Upholding their solemn oath to each other to keep the group going, Williams and Franklin began rebuilding the group, a process they would repeat over and over in the years to come.

With Paul Williams unlikely to recover from his illness any time soon, while travelling with the group, Richard Street was encouraged to begin learning the group's routines, and, as he told writer Gerri Hirshey, he felt like a 'buzzard' waiting in the wings. He told Hirshey that it 'was rough, Paul was there, but Paul was sick half the time, so he would just be moving his mouth while I would be singing his part from the wings.' Once it became clear Paul couldn't carry on any longer, Street was officially in. Decades later, Street was somewhat more nonchalant about the situation leading to his joining the group, telling the *Tampa Bay Times,* 'I just considered it returning to my rightful place. If things had been different early on, I would have been there from day one.' Paul Williams did take part in some of the sessions for *Solid Rock*, but was uncredited on the album itself.

The search for a replacement for Eddie Kendricks proved more of a challenge. They'd originally hired Ricky Owens to fill in, but he was quickly dropped after forgetting the lyrics to 'Just My Imagination' during an early performance. The group then hired a young singer called Otis Damon Harris (who went by Damon), who had been in a group called 'The Young Tempts', essentially a tribute act to The Temptations, but one that had recorded for The Isley Brothers' T-Neck Records. Harris was a solid choice: he was energetic, handsome and he sounded very similar to Eddie Kendricks. In an interview with *Blues & Soul*, Harris said:

> The Temptations had been the biggest major influence on me. I always listened to them and I always said I wanted to be like them in respect of being an entertainer and being able to perform like they always did. I just never ever thought I was going to be where I was, but I was very proud.

While the lineup changed, Norman Whitfield was still in control of the musical direction of the group. The production itself follows in the footsteps of the more experimental tracks on *Sky's The Limit* and sets the direction for the following albums, with longer album cuts that feature less vocals from The Temptations themselves. The instrumentation throughout is largely sparse on the A-side, conveying tension and a darkness, undoubtedly reflecting the context of America at the time, with the continuation of the bloody Vietnam War and inner city decline and deindustrialisation, symbolised by the rapid deterioration of Detroit itself.

Whitfield continued with his experimentation, resulting in longer songs, featuring slightly less psychedelic influences than previous albums but with more emphasis on pure funk. He also continued his habit of re-recording his own compositions with different artists and with a variety of arrangements and moods; it meant he didn't have to write anything new, and, perhaps cynically, meant he'd get paid royalties regardless.

Overall, *Solid Rock* is a decent effort from a group in flux: the new members had done their best to fit into the group, navigating the challenge of being, essentially, The Temptations 2.0, and Whitfield was forging ahead with his brand of psychedelic and experimental soul.

'Take A Look Around' (Barrett Strong, Norman Whitfield)

Solid Rock opens with a sparsely instrumented track that introduces this new lineup of The Temptations. All the members, bar Franklin, are given lines to sing, perhaps a deliberate choice by Whitfield to introduce the new talent of Street and Harris to their audience.

The song invites the listener to take a look around at the brutal inner-city life in America, where 'junk men' stand on the corner and the streets are unsafe to walk on. With the move to the suburbs by wealthier, white Americans, the inner cities in America were going through a period of rapid decline, no more so than Detroit, and Whitfield and Strong clearly drew on this here. Indeed, they're concerned for the future generations, yet unlike on 'Unite The World' on *Sky's The Limit*, they are more pessimistic about the future and offer no solution to these problems. A depressing start to *Solid Rock*, the rest of the album is, thankfully, not quite as bleak.

'Ain't No Sunshine' (Bill Withers)
Unlike Michael Jackson's cover of the Bill Withers classic on his debut solo album at Motown, The Temptations' version is a complete reworking of the song. The Temptations open the song backed by a repeating guitar riff, while they repeat the phrase 'ain't no sunshine' for two of the seven minutes of the song. Then, finally, the band fall in behind, and there's an extended keyboard solo, which lasts for over 90 seconds, before, finally, the lead vocal begins.

Street is given the first lead, and while he lacks the relaxed, earnest tone of Bill Withers, he does an impressive job. Edwards is given the 'I know, I know, I know' section before the lead switches to Harris, who sounds remarkably like Eddie Kendricks here. It's a much darker reading of the soul classic than the original, but certainly one of the more interesting of the numerous covers.

'Stop The War Now' (Barrett Strong, Norman Whitfield)
Given Berry Gordy's opposition to recording message songs, particularly given his resistance to Marvin Gaye's *What's Going On* and The Temptations' own version of 'War', it's remarkable that the group included this on *Solid Rock*. Originally recorded by Edwin Starr in 1970, it was an attempt by Whitfield to continue the success of Starr's version of 'War' – but this is even more lyrically explicit. Starr's version is essentially 'War, Part 2', beginning with the sounds of bombs being dropped and exploding before Starr begins his trademark growls and hollers and the backing singers chant 'stop the war, now!'

On *Solid Rock*, though, Whitfield creates a dark, cinematic soundscape complete with wah-wah guitar and the sound of soldiers marching, with the repeated chant of 'Does anyone give a damn/About the soldiers in Vietnam', while Melvin Franklin continually recites the first line from The Lord's Prayer.

The song stretches to an unheard-of 12 minutes, and it isn't until the four-minute mark that Dennis Edwards begins the verse. The lyrics are naturally pro-peace, but it's still pretty dark:

War casualties pile up each day
Cemeteries are overflowing
The leaders of the world claim victory's near
But the death list keeps right on growing
And what does a mother get in return
For the life of the son she's lost
A few measly pennies a month
A medal, a grave and a doggone cross

Right: Psychedelic-era Temptations: Dennis Edwards, Otis Williams, Paul Williams, Eddie Kendricks, Melvin Franklin. (*Getty*)

Left: Producer Norman Whitfield was crucial to The Temptations' changing sound and kept the hits coming despite changes in personnel. (*Getty*)

Left: *All Directions* (1972) featured the full 12-minute-long version of 'Papa Was A Rolling Stone'. (*Gordy/Motown*)

Right: With fewer but longer songs, The Temptations had grown frustrated working with Whitfield by the time *Masterpiece* (1973) was released. (*Gordy/Motown*)

Left: *1990* (1973) was the last full album to be produced by Norman Whitfield for The Temptations. (*Gordy/Motown*)

Right: Featuring blistering funk and epic ballads, *A Song For You* (1975) is one of The Temptations' finest efforts. (*Gordy/Motown*)

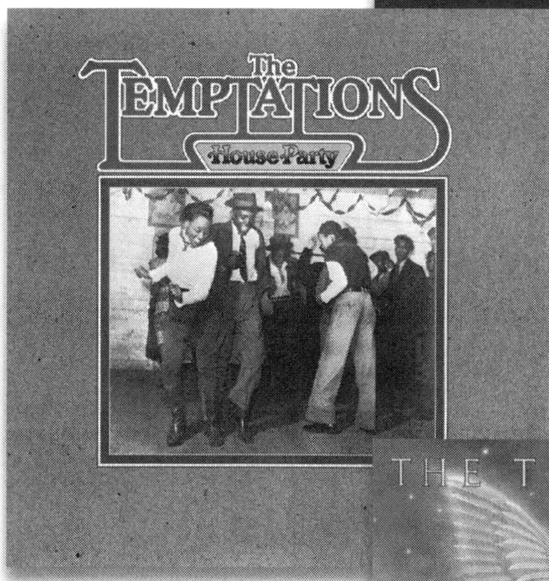

Left: Made up of outtakes from previous sessions, The Temptations disliked *House Party* (1975) immensely. (*Gordy/Motown*)

Right: *Wings Of Love* (1976) was essentially a Dennis Edwards solo record, produced by Jeffrey Bowen. (*Gordy/Motown*)

Left: The Temptations at the Millrun Playhouse Theater in the Round, Niles, Illinois, in 1976. (*Alamy*)

Below: Atlantic Records era lineup: Glenn Leonard, Melvin Franklin, Richard Street, Louis Price, Otis Williams. Photo taken from the rear sleeve of the *Hear To Tempt You* album. (*Atlantic*)

A far cry from the romantic ballads that The Temptations started out with, it begs the question of whether Gordy bothered listening to it before release, or if he simply trusted Whitfield's judgement that this wouldn't hurt the group's image. Most likely, he was distracted by his plans to move Motown's operations from Detroit to Los Angeles. Equally possible is Gordy's growing disinterest in the group in the face of lineup changes.

'What It Is?' (Barrett Strong, Norman Whitfield)
Opening in a similar vein to Marvin Gaye's 'What's Going On', with the sounds of voices at a gathering, perhaps even a party, 'What Is It?' is a much funkier track with more confusing lyrics, many of them simply repeating the line 'What is it? Sure is funky', which the track certainly is, although it's hard to know what the song is about. The phrase itself – 'what it is?' – was a street-greeting in the 1960s; the repeated response – 'sure is funky' – isn't really a response at all, suggesting perhaps there is no deeper meaning to the song – it's just a funk-workout.

Edwards vocalises throughout, with Harris and Street answering back. In one section, Street mimics a child, singing 'Children shouldn't play with bombs', and the rest of the group sing 'boom, boom, boom' in reply, contrasting with the up-tempo, danceable funk of the track itself. Could this be a comment on the deaths of children as collateral damage in the Vietnam War? Or is it a metaphor for something else? Perhaps it acts as a metaphorical warning towards those wishing for a revolution in America. Street even acknowledges the oddity of the lyrics, warning the listener, 'Don't try to figure out what this song is about'. Harris replies, 'Ooh yeah, just put it on your box when you're feeling down and out', suggesting that the song does lack meaning.

Whitfield clearly thought the track had potential, though, as he later recorded a version with the Undisputed Truth on their *Face To Face With The Truth* album, also released in 1972.

'Smooth Sailing (From Now On)' (Barrett Strong, Norman Whitfield)
In his autobiography, Williams claimed that Whitfield's aversion to recording ballads during this time was the root cause of tension between him and the group, but in reality, Whitfield did allow The Temptations some romantic moments on the otherwise harsh, message-oriented albums he was crafting. 'Smooth Sailing' is one such song, and could be as much about The Temptations as a fictional relationship: were Strong and Whitfield really writing about a loving, calm relationship, or was it a metaphor for the group's inner turmoil? With the new additions in the group, would it be smooth sailing? Of course, the answer would be no, but that wasn't clear to anyone at the time.

Harris is given the lead and does a masterful job; he sounds like Kendricks, there's no denying, this being one of his highlights during his stint with The

Temptations. It's almost dreamlike, contrasting with the relentless darkness of the first three songs on *Solid Rock*.

Interestingly, the backing track is the exact same as on The Monitors' version of 'Too Busy Thinking About My Baby'; Whitfield simply recycled it for 'Smooth Sailing'. Like so many of the songs recorded by The Monitors, it would only later be released on *Say You! The Motown Anthology 1963 – 1968* in 2011, featuring Street on lead.

'Superstar (Remember How You Got Where You Are)' (Barrett Strong, Norman Whitfield)

In the liner notes to their *Gold* greatest hits collection, Williams claimed that Whitfield had originally written 'Superstar' 'about a friend of his, a producer ... but it became something deeper as we worked through it – it grew into a message to David and Eddie.' Indeed, you didn't need to be a genius to work out who the lyrics were aimed at.

A raging, pounding rump of funk, the piano-led 'Superstar' takes aim at these ex-Temptations, with Strong's lyrics taking no prisoners. The Funk Brothers create an intense rhythm track, aided by a dramatic, siren-like horn arrangement by Paul Riser. Whitfield uses his trick of having all The Temptations, bar Williams, trade the lead, reminding the former members of the group in a less-than-friendly tone to 'remember how you got where you are'.

The lines 'Enjoy your champagne and caviar/And your chauffeur drivin' fancy car' are clearly aimed at Ruffin, who travelled in his own personalised limousine while touring with the group, causing resentment among the others. Meanwhile, when Kendricks left the group, he made his displeasure of his later time in the group known and would disparage the new lineup of Temptations while launching his solo career. Later on, he even told Williams and Franklin that the group should have disbanded when he and Paul Williams departed. Strong uses 'Superstar' to fire back, writing the lyric 'Bridges, don't burn 'em behind you' in response.

Released as a single in October 1971, 'Superstar' was a hit for the re-constituted group, hitting number 18 on the pop charts and number eight on the R&B charts. It proved, for now at least, that the group could weather the storm as the public continued to buy their records, even with a substantially different lineup.

Given the song's animosity towards him, Ruffin covered the song on his 1975 album, *Me 'N' Rock And Roll Are Here To Stay.* Either he wasn't offended by the song, or perhaps the album's producer, one Norman Whitfield, selected it for him to record as a joke.

Whatever the reason for covering it, Ruffin's version isn't very good. For reasons known only to Whitfield, his version is smothered with fake audience noise and applause that almost drowns out Ruffin's vocal, making it almost unlistenable.

'It's Summer' (Barrett Strong, Norman Whitfield)

The Temptations originally recorded 'It's Summer' for their *Psychedelic Shack* album, and here Whitfield takes the unusual step of re-recording it.

On the first version, Franklin, who speaks the lyrics, is given a rare lead, but here, Edwards is given the lead, although he sings unusually high and soft, showcasing a different dimension to his voice compared to his usual gnarl. He's aided by some delightful backing vocals, anchored by Franklin. The track features some uncredited vocals from Paul Williams, who recorded it before his departure from the group, and also before Harris joined. This version has a lo-fi feel compared to the *Psychedelic Shack* version, which places greater emphasis on those exquisite vocals.

Yet, despite the performance of the group, when released as a single in June 1971, it failed to break the top 40 on the pop charts, the first time a single from the group failed to break through since 1963.

'The End Of Our Road' (Barrett Strong, Norman Whitfield, Roger Penzabene)

Written before his death in 1967, 'The End Of Our Road' was a holdover from a previous collaboration between Strong and Whitfield and the lyricist Roger Penzabene. While it's an up-tempo, almost danceable track, it shares the same theme as 'I Wish It Would Rain', which Penzabene also wrote the lyrics for: a woman causing her man intense heartbreak. His unhappiness continued to provide the inspiration for excellent material, even if his professional success didn't translate into personal triumph. In this story, the woman in question is 'Runnin' around with every guy in town', leading the narrator to conclude that he's 'sick and tired of your stuff', although, simultaneously, he's sad about the relationship ending.

All Directions (1972)

Personnel:
Otis Williams, Melvin Franklin, Dennis Edwards, Richard Street, Damon Harris: vocals
Billy Cooper, Joe Messina, Melvin 'Wah Wah' Ragin, Robert Ward, Paul Warren, Robert White, Eddie Willis: guitar
Richard 'Pistol' Allen, Uriel Jones, Aaron Smith, Andrew Smith: drums
Earl Van Dyke: piano
Johnny Griffith: organ
Bob Babbitt, James Jamerson, Leroy Taylor: bass
Jack Ashford: tambourine, maracas, sticks
Jack Brokensha: timpani, vibes, bells, gourd
Eddie 'Bongo' Brown: bongo, conga
Paul Riser: arrangements, conducting
Produced at Hitsville USA, Detroit, by Norman Whitfield between March and June 1972
Mastering engineers: Norman Whitfield, Orson Wells
Label: Gordy
Release date: 27 July 1972
Length: 34:37
Charts: US pop: 2, US R&B: 1, UK: 19

By the time The Temptations set about recording the follow-up to *Solid Rock*, Whitfield was no longer working with his lyricist, Barrett Strong. The split was a surprise to the group, who were unsure what had happened between them, but suddenly, Strong was no longer around. Around this time, he would try to rekindle his solo career, signing with Capital Records to release two albums in 1975 and 1976. Both are long out of print.

For The Temptations, however, this meant that Whitfield was now in complete control, but it also meant he had little new material to work with, other than 'Papa Was A Rolling Stone' and 'Funky Music Sho Nuff Turns Me On'. Therefore, Whitfield resorted to re-recording several of his compositions for other artists with the group, along with several covers. As a result, *All Directions* ended up being what Williams called a 'truly strange mix of tunes', from the political to the romantic, with Whitfield continuing with his unique mix of soul, funk and psychedelia. However, it's one of the group's better efforts, a consistently good album that lacks more filler than previous albums, even if there are fewer, longer tracks overall.

Whitfield recorded the bulk of the tracks with the Funk Brothers, assisted by others, most notably Melvin 'Wah-Wah' Ragin, whose funk-meets-psychedelia guitar playing reaches its apex on 'Papa Was A Rolling Stone'. This would become more pronounced on The Temptations' next album, *Masterpiece*.

Despite the concerns within the group regarding Whitfield's experiments and control over their musical direction – Williams recalled thinking the album and the singles would bomb on release – *All Directions* went on to become one of their biggest-selling albums, shifting over half a million copies and hitting number two and number one on the US R&B and pop charts, respectively. It also reached number 19 on the UK Albums Chart, making it their highest-charting non-greatest hits album. Given the tumultuous year The Temptations had with personnel changes and rising tensions with Whitfield, *All Directions* is an impressive effort from a group many had now written off with the departures of Eddie Kendricks and Paul Williams.

Yet, it also consolidated further Whitfield's hold over them: The Temptations might have found his control in the studio infuriating, but they couldn't deny his genius nor his ability to give them hits. For the next two albums, without Strong's influence or writing, it would be Whitfield alone who wrote and produced the songs, regardless of what anyone else thought. This stubbornness proved costly in the months to come.

'Funky Music Sho Nuff Turns Me On' (Barrett Strong, Norman Whitfield)
This was originally recorded by Edwin Starr in 1971 after the success of 'War'. It was another R&B hit for Starr, reaching number six on the R&B charts, although it was less successful on the pop charts, peaking at number 64, suggesting his brand of fiery singing wasn't suited to more mainstream white audiences. Given Whitfield's falling out with Strong and therefore a lack of material ready to record with The Temptations, it no doubt made sense for Whitfield to have another crack at recording the song for *All Directions* in the hope it might be a bigger hit, or at the very least, would bulk out the album. Indeed, The Temptations' version isn't so much of an improvement on Starr's version as it is just another version, neither better nor worse.

For The Temptations' version, Whitfield attempts to make it sound like a 'live' track, piping in audience noise and an MC welcoming the group – it's not clear if this is an actual live track, or one recorded to sound so in the studio. The track begins with the sound of a crowd being warmed up for a Temptations show before the instrumentation fades in over 'audience' applause. Street and Harris sing the first verse, trading lines, before the other Temptations fall in behind. Everyone gets to trade lead, while the others harmonise behind them. However, despite Whitfield's attempts to make this sound like a live recording, the mix is a bit cluttered and the voices are somewhat lost in the instrumentation, but it's nonetheless incredibly funky and the horns could have been pinched from a Sly & The Family Stone session.

It was released as the B-side to the album's first single, 'Mother Nature', with this flip-side also charting, hitting number 27 on the US R&B charts.

'Run Charlie Run' (C. Maurice King, Jan Forman)
One of the most controversial songs recorded by the group, it was one they didn't really want to record. Although not written by Whitfield or Strong,

Whitfield clearly felt strongly about recording it for *All Directions*. In his memoir, Williams recounted that while the group didn't have any qualms about the song's story, which discusses white Americans fleeing a recently integrated neighbourhood (known as the 'white flight', whereby white families moved from the inner cities to the suburbs), continuing a theme present on *Solid Rock*, it was the racial slur that Whitfield added to the chorus they disagreed with. After the line 'Run, Charlie Run', Whitfield had the group sing, 'The niggers are coming, the niggers are coming', in what Williams called 'the incredulous tone of voice Norman must have thought white people would use.' Eventually, the group caved and recorded it, though they never performed it on stage.

'Papa Was A Rolling Stone' (Barrett Strong, Norman Whitfield)
Originally recorded by The Undisputed Truth and released in May 1973, Whitfield, presumably not fully satisfied with the result, and lacking any new material, decided to revisit it with The Temptations. The Undisputed Truth's version is more rock-oriented and has a much more cluttered arrangement than that used for The Temptations; it later appeared on their album *Law Of The Land* in 1973 (the title song was also recorded by both groups, both versions again being produced by Whitfield). The song tells the story of an absent father from the perspective of a child asking his mother who he really was, with the mother replying he was a 'rolling stone' who died, leaving them 'all alone'.

According to Williams, Whitfield created the instrumental track while the group were on the road performing, and when they first heard the tracks, they knew he was onto something special – but for another artist. They did not want to record it. He wrote in his autobiography: 'We were just so damned sick of that type of song. We begged to go back to ballads, but nobody was listening to us.' Whitfield, though, could not be persuaded to shelve the track, and eventually persuaded the group to record their vocals.

There was also, at least according to Williams and immortalised in *The Temptations* TV miniseries, an argument between Whitfield and Edwards, with the latter angry with the song's lyrics:

It was the third of September
That day I'll always remember, yes I will
'Cause that was the day that my daddy died

On Williams' account, Edwards was annoyed because his father had died on 3 September, and took it personally, resulting in him delivering the lead vocal 'through clenched teeth'. According to Edwards, though, that wasn't quite the truth: he told the *Detroit Free Press* that his father, a preacher, actually died on 3 October, although that was a little close for comfort. But what was true is that Whitfield did annoy Edwards and the group during the recording sessions. Edwards told *The Free Press*:

> I wanted to put more on it. I didn't want it to be so bland. But [Whitfield] actually wanted it bland. Every time I would try to oversing it, he would change it. He would make me mad.

There was method in Whitfield's madness: by riling Edwards up, he was able to get the lead vocal he wanted for 'Papa', one that was restrained but more angry and terse. The song opens with the bassline, repeated beneath a hi-hat and a dark, cinematic string arrangement written by Paul Riser. When he first heard the rhythm track, Riser wasn't impressed, but the more he listened to it, he felt it conveyed a sense of mystery, and using the soundtrack to the film *Shaft* by Isaac Hayes as an influence, he arranged the strings like a film score: the strings play long, sustained notes creating an eerie and suspenseful atmosphere, soundtracking the drama that plays out in the lyrics.

Using musicians from the Detroit Symphony Orchestra, Riser's arrangement added a new level of suspense to Whitfield's sparse rhythm track. Whitfield then had Melvin 'Wah-Wah' Ragin add his trademark guitar playing to the track, along with a mournful trumpet solo from Maurice Davis, with a new tool that gave his trumpet an echo, which Riser later described in the book *Anatomy Of A Song* as sounding like 'kids crying or a police siren – a shrill flavour from the streets.'

Edwards sings the first verse solo, but in the second verse, he shares with Franklin and Street before Street and Harris sing the third verse between them. All the vocals mirror Edwards' angry, gritty vocal, and the chorus is repeated several times over.

Due to the song's length, almost 12 minutes long, Motown issued two single versions, one reaching almost seven minutes and a shorter five-minute version. Not that the group thought it would do much at any rate, they'd left the studio furious with Whitfield over their treatment, predicting it would flop and hoping they could get back to the business of recording ballads. Fortunately, their predictions were wrong: 'Papa' was a number-five R&B hit, but a number-one US pop smash, and won the Grammy in 1974 for 'Best R&B Vocal Performance By a Duo, Group or Chorus' and for 'Best R&B Instrumental Performance'. Live versions appeared on their *In Japan!* album, as well as on the soundtrack to the concert-film *Save The Children* (the latter album, released in 1973, has never been reissued).

It eventually became one of their signature songs, proving once again that this new lineup were worthy of continuing on The Temptations name.

'Love Woke Me Up This Morning' (Nikolas Ashford, Valerie Simpson)
Written by the husband and wife duo Ashford and Simpson, 'Love Woke Me Up This Morning' was first released on Marvin Gaye and Tammi Terrell's *Easy* album in 1969. Simpson did her own version on her solo album for Motown in 1971, and an early version of hers appeared on the Motown collection *Unreleased 1967* in 2017. It's this version from 1967 that Whitfield essentially

borrows from for The Temptations' arrangement, which is a little cleaner perhaps, reflecting the improvements in Motown's recording abilities and the resources available at Whitfield's disposal. Plus, given Barrett Strong's break with Whitfield, he probably had few other original songs to work with.

Here, Harris takes the lead, delivering a soft, sweet lead vocal that contrasts with the heavy funk of 'Papa Was A Rolling Stone', as if Whitfield was proving a point to both the group and their audience that he could still provide ballads when it suited him. The arrangement is dominated by some jazz-style drumming, a big string arrangement and some exquisite piano playing from Earl Van Dyke. The backing vocals are minimal, and although not listed on the album, it certainly sounds like female voices (perhaps the Andantes) were used rather than the rest of The Temptations. But their equally soft vocals work well with Harris's lead, creating one of his finest recordings with the group.

'I Ain't Got Nothin'' (C. Maurice King, Evans King)
An intensely bleak, despairing song, 'I Ain't Got Nothin'' tells the story of a man who has nothing: no love, no money and no future. It features a rare lead from Williams, whose straightforward vocal works perfectly with the moody, almost depressing, arrangement written by Riser. It's heavy on the mournful-sounding strings, which Williams matches with his equally morose vocal. Williams might not have been the strongest lead singer in the group, but his approach here sounds like an ordinary man bemoaning his bad luck. He's helped by Franklin and Street, who sing a couple of lead lines and the backing vocals in a doo-wop style that harks back to their time in The Distants, and they sound equally as sorrowful as they repeat 'I ain't got nothing'.

The lyrics are childlike on first examination, even quirky, as the protagonist lists objects that belong with other objects, acting as a metaphor for love. Take the second verse, for example, and the selection of objects chosen:

> Every stove has a fire
> And every car has a tire
> Every fish has a bowl, and every shoe has a sole
> Everybody, everybody's got something but me
> I ain't got nothing

Clearly, this is a man in desperate need of affection, comparing himself to a fish without a bowl. Thankfully, the lyrics improve in the bridge as the story becomes clearer – the protagonist craves love and to be loved:

> Now I don't care about politics
> And things across the sea (Across the sea)
> All I wanna to do is love

And have somebody love me
I need, I need somebody

The arrangement and vocals from The Temptations save the song from its lyrics, making it a worthwhile listen at least once.

'The First Time Ever (I Saw Your Face)' (Ewan MacColl)
Written by Ewan MacColl for his future wife and singer Peggy Seeger, it was popularised by Roberta Flack, who recorded it on her debut album *First Take* in 1969; it became a hit for her in 1971 after Clint Eastwood used it in his film, *Play Misty For Me*. Here, we get to hear the song from a male perspective, with Whitfield giving the lead to Street, whose mellow vocal here is softer and thinner than Flack's, but at points, he seems to struggle reaching the higher notes. Nevertheless, it's possibly his best studio performance as a Temptation. Whitfield matches Street's whispering vocal with a sparsely orchestrated track that never overpowers Street's performance; the piano and bass move the track along, while the strings are added lightly in the choruses. In fact, it's nearly a Street solo song; it's not until the end of the song when the rest of the group repeat 'your face' in response that they make their presence known. Even then, the backing vocals are mixed low, so as not to overwhelm Street's lead. This was not simply a run-of-the-mill cover that Motown previously used as 'filler' on their earlier albums; this was one of Street's most triumphant moments as a Temptation.

'Mother Nature' (Nick Zesses, Dino Fekaris)
Returning to the cinematic approach, 'Mother Nature' is a ballad in tribute to the power of the natural world. Edwards sings the lead, beginning his vocal softly, backed by just Earl Van Dyke on the piano, along with bass and drums, before Riser's horn arrangement kicks in and the rest of the group begin harmonising. It's less moody than 'I Ain't Got Nothing', but it's equally mournful, a prayer perhaps for a world which was trying to tame Mother Nature without fully appreciating her awesome force. The song builds the longer it goes on, with Edwards returning to his gospel-shouting, and the horn and string arrangements gather intensity.

Oddly, Motown released this as the first single from *All Directions* on 1 June 1972, backed with 'Funky Music Sho Nuff Turns Me On'. The release was not a huge success, reaching just number 27 on the US R&B chart and just number 92 on the pop charts. It may well have been this performance on the charts that unnerved Williams and the group, leading them to conclude that *All Directions* was a dud.

'Do Your Thing' (Isaac Hayes)
Written and recorded by Isaac Hayes for his soundtrack to the film *Shaft*, a classic of the emerging blaxploitation genre of film scores, Haye's original

album version ran to 19 minutes, something that clearly impressed Whitfield (for The Temptations' next album, *Masterpiece*, the title track stretched to nearly 15 minutes, although Stax did release a single edit running to just over three minutes). Yet, the version he produced for *All Directions* is an impressively short 3:30, in which he keeps Hayes' cinematic feel, but with a slightly slower tempo.

Riser gives Whitfield another dramatic horn arrangement, not completely different to Hayes' version; the playing on both is raw and made up of short, stabbing phrases that punctuate the groove. It's moodier than the original, although not as gritty. That is compounded by the decision to give Street the bulk of the lead, whose vocal style is almost the opposite of Hayes's deep baritone, which is far more sensual than Street's lighter and smoother tenor. Street's soft style of singing is aided by Harris's tenor dominating the harmonies, although Franklin is given a couple of lines to rumble through for good measure, and the latter half of the song has the group simply repeat the line 'do it right/do your thing'.

As a result, 'Do Your Thing' is not simply a note-by-note cover of Hayes' original but a respectable effort to close out an overall excellent album.

Masterpiece (1973)

Personnel:
Otis Williams, Melvin Franklin, Dennis Edwards, Richard Street, Damon Harris: vocals
Robert Ward, Melvin 'Wah Wah' Watson, Joe Messina, Paul Warren, Robert White, Eddie Willis: guitar
Aaron Smith, Richard 'Pistol' Allen, Uriel Jones, Andrew Smith: drums
Leroy Taylor, Bob Babbitt, Eddie Watkins: bass
Johnny Griffith, Earl Van Dyke: organ
Eddie 'Bongo' Brown: bongos, congas
Jack Ashford: tambourine, maracas, sticks
Maurice Davis: trumpet
Ted Lucas: harmonica
Jack Brokensha: timpani, vibes, bells, gourd
Produced at Hitsville USA, Detroit, by Norman Whitfield between September 1972 and January 1973
Engineer: Orson Lewis
Mastering: Norman Whitfield, Orson Lewis
Label: Gordy
Release date: 21 February 1973
Length: 42:08
Charts: US R&B: 1, US Pop: 7, UK: 28

Masterpiece followed the direction laid down on *All Directions*: more instrumentation, fewer vocals and longer but fewer tracks. It was the group's last album recorded in Detroit at the famed Motown/Hitsville Studios before the label finally moved all operations to Los Angeles.

By this point, relations between The Temptations and Norman Whitfield were hurtling towards a breaking point; this was their penultimate album with Whitfield as sole producer. In his autobiography, Williams claimed that the group had begun pleading with Whitfield to include more ballads on their albums and fewer heavy, longer experimental tracks. But Whitfield refused to bow to this pressure, although in fairness to him, *Masterpiece* did open with the beautiful ballad 'Hey Girl (I Like Your Style)'. If that wasn't enough to anger the group, the album artwork also seemed to demean their efforts: the front cover features a sculpture by Parvis Sadighian of The Temptations lined up, side-by-side, while the back cover has a large picture of Norman Whitfield looking contemplative, above a much smaller picture of The Temptations themselves, performing on stage, slightly out of focus. The album notes even give a 'special thank you from Whitfield and The Temptations for the musicians who provided their time and talents in the production of *Masterpiece*', as if the group was purely the creation of Whitfield, the leader. It was no wonder the group were asking themselves whether this was a Temptations record, or a Norman Whitfield record that they were simply the guest vocalists on.

Whitfield, though, was unrepentant; he was the producer, and he would decide the musical direction of the album alone. On *Masterpiece*, he wrote and produced all the tracks alone. Quoted in Graham Betts's *Motown Encyclopaedia* years later, Whitfield had softened his stance, but only just, saying:

> I wanted to try some songs that had the scope and feeling of a movie. The group had some scepticism about taking on the material ... Look, trends were changing and I was only interested in keeping them on top and keeping them current. A transition was needed, but I admit I never really confided in them as to what I was doing.

His stubbornness, though, was rapidly bringing to an end their so far successful collaboration. What had once seemed like a perfect match was now disintegrating and, as time would prove, The Temptations' abilities to have hit records. Yet, at the time, and even with the distance of time, Williams maintained he was right, writing later that, 'on some tracks, our singing seemed to function as ornamentation for Norman's instrumental incursions.' It wasn't just Williams who was annoyed at the situation; even Dennis Edwards, who benefited the most from Whitfield's psychedelic and cinematic soul, was frustrated with Whitfield. Bett's quotes him saying that 'I just wish we had the opportunity to do more vocally on the album. I just don't think we did enough.'

In fairness to Whitfield, those 'instrumental incursions', as Williams describes them, were, by and large, majestic. His determination to push new sounds and boundaries of what he could record and get away with resulted in some excellent recordings: the title track is a cinematic adventure into urban America, while tracks like 'Law Of The Land' became early influences in the emerging disco genre. His gritty and political tracks reflected the turmoil of America in the early 1970s, but after years of singing such songs, The Temptations wanted to return to something softer, allowing their fans to escape the nation's troubles, not get lost in them.

Credit for the brilliant arrangements on *Masterpiece* must also go to Paul Riser, who himself was shocked at the length of some of the music Whitfield had written, but nonetheless created some excellent arrangements without which *Masterpiece* would have failed.

Whitfield later told Sharon Davis:

> I admit I literally had to beg them to record their last three albums that they did for me. And they became their biggest. They went gold and were selling 750,000 albums each time. My favourite was *Masterpiece* because there was so much behind-the-scenes work put into that. The whole direction, though, was deliberately planned and was what I like to term a natural growth of my own personal identity.

These professional challenges corresponded with more personal problems for former member Paul Williams. Almost six months after the release of *Masterpiece*, Williams was found dead in his car a few blocks from Motown. His death was ruled a suicide by a gunshot wound to the head. With his health still an issue, he had continued to drink heavily. He had invested in a fashion store which had gone broke, he owed the IRS taxes and his solo career hadn't taken off. He missed being a Temptation and performing with his friends and had expressed thoughts of suicide to both Williams and Franklin. Although Motown continued to keep him on the payroll and even recorded a few singles with him, they were never released in his lifetime. Somewhat prophetically, one of those songs was titled 'Feel Like Giving Up' and was released decades after his death.

'Hey Girl (I Like Your Style)' (Norman Whitfield)

Perhaps Whitfield finally gave into to The Temptations concerns by allowing them to record this excellent ballad as the album's opener, but it's the only one on *Masterpiece*, and it's the only song on the album that gives the listener any break from the depressing tales of black American life. In fact, you could question why it was on *Masterpiece* at all, given that its lyrics are so different from the rest of the songs.

Richard Street is given the lead and delivers another fine performance on this beautiful, soft ballad. Street gives a similar performance to his lead on 'The First Time I Ever Saw Your Face' on *All Directions*; on 'Hey Girl', he begins almost in a whisper before his voice builds in intensity as the song progresses. So, too, does the instrumentation and orchestration, with Paul Riser writing a string arrangement that begins softly before building to a dramatic climax.

'Hey Girl' was the third and final single to be released from *Masterpiece*, hitting number two on the R&B charts, but reaching only number 35 on the pop charts. It would become part of their concerts, too, and a version was released on their *In Japan!* live album in 1974.

'Masterpiece' (Norman Whitfield)

How could Whitfield top 'Papa Was A Rolling Stone'? The answer, at least in his mind, was 'Masterpiece', a 14-minute cinematic odyssey into the realism and strife of the inner city. Undoubtedly, the song is a masterpiece, but more so for Whitfield than The Temptations themselves. Already tired of singing about social and political issues, the group also disliked Whitfield's ongoing attempts to lengthen their songs, resulting in fewer individual songs per album. The group were worried that they were ripping their fans off, undoing years of hard work in building and maintaining an audience. Whitfield could not be told otherwise, though, and 'Masterpiece' comes in at 13:50. However, the group only sing on the track for less than three minutes.

There's no doubt that Whitfield outdid himself on the production, clearly influenced by the Blaxploitation film genre and their gritty soundtracks, and the pioneering cinematic soul of Isaac Hayes. Hayes's songs were getting longer, too; his 1969 album *Hot Buttered Soul* – containing only four songs, including an unheard-of 18-minute-long version of 'By The Time I Get To Phoenix' – set the trend of these elongated musical adventures. Whitfield drew on this in the years that followed, pushing boundaries even further. It's remarkable that only several years earlier, Motown was still primarily a singles company, with its songs designed to be three-minute hits.

Yet, 'Masterpiece' pushed Whitfield's boundaries further, combining heavy percussion, eerie string and horn arrangements and plenty of wah-wah guitar, courtesy of Melvin Ragin, better known as Wah-Wah Watson for his guitar chops. This combination creates an urban soundscape in which themes of urban decay, poverty and crime are all explored, reflecting the state of Detroit in the early 1970s as a symbol of post-industrialisation. It's no coincidence that this was the final album The Temptations recorded in the city. Yet, 'Masterpiece' also foreshadowed the dominance of the producer in the emerging disco trend, which would peak later in the decade. Disco was largely a producer's genre: they would craft their own musical masterpiece, focusing primarily on the instrumentation and often epic arrangements, before simply finding someone to add vocals later. Whitfield was ahead of the curve then, and while 'Masterpiece' might not have been as danceable as disco, it's certainly a funky epic. But for a group known and loved for their vocal abilities, this approach was unlikely to work for The Temptations in the long run.

When The Temptations finally begin to sing, they tell the now classic story of the inner city experience: poverty, crime, drugs. It's all here, albeit condensed into minutes of vocals, while the dark arrangement creates an undercurrent of danger. Otis Williams gives a spoken introduction, something which would become his niche on later albums, while Damon Harris sings the first verse at the same time. Richard Street then takes the lead on the next three lines of the second verse, sharing the last line with Harris on some suitably depressing lyrics:

> Thousands of lives wasting away
> People living from day to day
> This is a challenge just staying alive
> 'Cause in the ghetto only the strong survive

The sharing of leads continues, with Harris sharing with Franklin, before Edwards sings the outro. Whitfield then circles back to 'Papa Was A Rolling Stone' with a similar horn arrangement around the nine-minute mark.

Despite the reservations of the group, a shorter single mix was released, and the song topped the US R&B singles charts and even reached number seven on the pop charts, but it was their last top ten pop single. They also continued performing it in concert for years to come, and it appears on their *In Japan!* live album (although shortened to a more accessible 2:31).

'Ma' (Norman Whitfield)
'Ma' is the counter piece to 'Papa Was A Rolling Stone', except the woman in this story provides and sacrifices for her family, rather than the deadbeat, rolling stone father. Set in the 'back woods of Mississippi', Ma has raised 16 children singlehandedly, living on a diet of moonshine and tobacco, and in the process of raising her brood, she has 'ruined her body'. When her husband died, she didn't love another, but played his guitar to keep his memory alive. It's a song of motherly love and sacrifice, and is a moodier, bluesier and simply more depressing version of the story in 'I'll Always Love My Mama' by The Intruders, which was released the same year as *Masterpiece*. Whitfield has Street sing the bulk of the lead, although Harris and Franklin also contribute, while the beat pounds along, with plenty of hi-hat drumming and even more wah-wah guitar, all brought together under another dark string arrangement.

'Law Of The Land' (Norman Whitfield)
Without the help of Barrett Strong to create new content, Whitfield once again recorded the same song with both The Temptations and The Undisputed Truth. The latter's version would be released as a single in June 1973, after The Temptations' own version had appeared on *Masterpiece*. The Undisputed Truth's version is faster than The Temptations', but it's still full of horns and wah-wah guitar. The Temptations' version straddles both funk and early disco, although the lyrics are much more socially conscious compared with the hedonist, escapist lyrics that disco would later be known for. Edwards sings the bulk of the lead, doing his best growls and gospel-influenced shouting throughout, before Harris takes over with his sweet falsetto.

Though not released as a single in America, it was released in the UK, peaking at number 41 on the singles chart. It would be their last appearance on the UK charts until 'Standing On The Top' nearly a decade later.

'Plastic Man' (Norman Whitfield)
Never one not to re-use a good idea, 'Plastic Man' does sound like a slightly sped-up version of 'Papa Was A Rolling Stone', as if he was remixing it for a disco, albeit with different lyrics. The subject of the song is a man who pretends to know everything, but really knows nothing at all: he's a 'self-preservationist', who takes but never lends, and whose ultimate fear is 'being just another face in the crowd'. He'd do anything to anyone to succeed. Whitfield could be writing about both the hangers-on to the famous and successful, or perhaps the famous themselves, who fear their fame won't last.

Released as the second single from *Masterpiece*, 'Plastic Man' struggled into the top 40 on the pop charts, but did better on the R&B charts, reaching number eight. Outside of the R&B market, it seemed that Whitfield's socially conscious soul was losing its appeal.

'Hurry Tomorrow' (Norman Whitfield)

The album ends with 'Hurry Tomorrow', which, despite its title, is another long track reaching over eight minutes. Whitfield returns to the theme of drug abuse and stages a sort of audio-play in which Street plays the role of a drug dealer, encouraging his friend, played by Harris, to take what he's offering to lighten the load, telling him, 'Dig it, man, you just take this and it's a brand new experience!' What then follows is a trip of epic proportions for Harris's character, giving him 'a feeling I've never felt before, in a room without a floor or door'. Harris begs for tomorrow to come and provide his escape from this epic trip of pain and confusion.

The narrator's experience is reflected in Whitfield's dark, yet sparse, production; clearly influenced by Curtis Mayfield's 'Pusherman' on the *Superfly* soundtrack, Whitfield gives us a much moodier, depressing and frightening take on the effect of drugs on America's youth. This is certainly a masterpiece, although it probably suited Whitfield's current mindset than that of The Temptations.

1990 (1973)

Personnel:
Otis Williams, Melvin Franklin, Dennis Edwards, Richard Street, Damon Harris: vocals
Melvin 'Wah Wah' Ragin (aka Watson), Dennis Coffey, Eddie Willis, Kenji Brown: guitar
James Jamerson, Ron Brown, Lequeint Jobe: bass
Jack Ashford: tambourine
Aaron Smith, Ed Greene, James Gadson, Henry Garner Jr: drums
Bobbye Hall, Terral W. Santiel: congas
Earl Van Dyke, Mark Davis, Victor Nix: keyboards
George Bohannon: trombone
Michael Moore: tenor saxophone
Fred Dunn, Kenneth Copeland: trumpet
Paul Riser: arrangements
Produced in Los Angeles, California, by Norman Whitfield in 1973
Engineers: Larry Miles, Art Stewart, Cal Harris, Russ Terrana
Mastering: Norman Whitfield, Russ Terrana
Label: Gordy
Release date: 7 December 1973
Length: 37:31
Charts: US pop: 19, US R&B: 2

Released just ten months after *Masterpiece*, *1990* was the last time Norman Whitfield produced The Temptations until they were reunited in 1983 for *Back To Basics*. Again, the pattern was similar to *Masterpiece* and *All Directions*; Whitfield was a stubborn man and was unlikely to bow to the group's wishes if he felt he was right, which he clearly did. In his memoirs, Williams wrote that, by the time they had recorded *1990*, which only has two songs on side two, 'we felt more strongly than ever that our fans were being ripped off.' After reading reviews of *Masterpiece* that called the group 'the Norman Whitfield Choral Singers', Williams knew their working relationship was over. These were supposed to be Temptations albums, after all.

The group took their concerns to Berry Gordy, who later recounted in his autobiography that Williams complained about Whitfield's behaviour and demanded a new producer for their next album. In his telling, Gordy could see both perspectives – but, as ever, it was the sales that counted:

> I agreed with Otis that Norman could be ridiculous, but I knew where he was coming from. He knew what he wanted and how to get it. That was his style, I reminded Otis, and his style was getting them hit after hit after hit.

But a compromise could not be found, and with the release of *1990*, the Whitfield-Temptations double act was over. As Gordy reflected later, while

The Temptations went on to work with a variety of writers and producers, including Gordy himself, 'none of us could give them the super hit power Norman had.'

Whitfield himself wasn't surprised by the group's decision but was disappointed not to be able to work with them again. He told Sharon Davis:

> I understood why they wanted to make the split [from working with me], due to the kind of changes groups go through and problems that were peculiar to them. So that was why I agreed to release them from their contract. Their friendship meant more to me than a piece of paper, and this way, there would be no undercurrent and we could stay friends. I would have liked to have carried on with them a little longer, but I'm not the type to beg.

These squabbles aside, *1990* is a lost gem unfairly overshadowed by *All Directions* and *Masterpiece*. Once again, Whitfield was in total control, writing and producing all seven tracks, with Paul Riser once again doing all the arrangements. This time, though, there are more ballads than *Masterpiece*, all featuring some excellent vocals from both Damon Harris and Richard Street. However, Whitfield couldn't bring himself to record just ballads; he wasn't going to give up his brand of cinematic soul that easily.

The album also features musicians from Whitfield's next big group, Rose Royce. Once he left Motown in 1975, he formed his own Whitfield Records and produced most of Rose Royce's hits – they became his biggest non-Motown success. As before, the lead vocals on *1990* are split, but Street certainly gets more airtime from Whitfield than before. Overall, then, *1990* is an excellent album, lost somewhat amongst the other Whitfield-produced material, but an album that's well worth revisiting to hear this lineup in their prime.

'Let Your Hair Down' (Norman Whitfield)

With Rose Royce providing the backing track, 'Let Your Hair Down' is a return to the hard-hitting, in-your-face R&B jams that Whitfield produced earlier for The Temptations, such as 'I Can't Get Next To You' or 'Superstar'. Edwards sings the lead vocal, opening the song with his trademark growl before beginning the first verse. The lyrics send a message to the straight-laced listener, to 'let their reputation sit a while', loosen up and let their hair down and, quite literally, get down. Unlike recent singles, this isn't a 'message song' as such, but a pure funk workout that makes you want to dance. Indeed, this is made easy by the funk that Rose Royce provide alongside the great horn arrangement.

It was another number one for the group on the US R&B charts when released as a single in November 1973, backed with 'Ain't No Justice', yet despite the song's strength, it only managed to reach number 27 on the pop charts. Reflecting on the song later, Williams wrote that he was 'surprised it went to number one – one of those things that hit a nerve at the time.'

'I Need You' (Norman Whitfield)
Opening with an almost Western feel, perfect for a soundtrack about a cowboy and his love interest, 'I Need You' is a lost Temptations gem. Whitfield returns to the cinematic soundscapes of his earlier work but manages to keep this mid-tempo ballad to within three minutes. For a ballad, it's plenty funky, and Whitfield manages to cram a lot into three minutes. There's a brooding string section along with another excellent horn arrangement by Paul Riser, all driven along by a pounding bassline and Melvin 'Wah-Wah' Ragin's guitar – there's even room for a short keyboard solo.

Harris sings lead and delivers a fine performance, sounding less like Eddie Kendricks and more like himself; after several years of being a Temptation, Harris was beginning to sound more natural and comfortable with his position in the group.

'Heavenly' (Norman Whitfield)
Released as the second single from *1990* in February 1974, it managed to reach number eight on the R&B charts but only reached number 43 on the pop charts. Street recalled 'Heavenly' as one of the major disappointments in his career as a Temptation. In his memoir, he blamed the song's failure on the charts on Ewart Abner, who had become Motown president in 1973. According to Street, when Abner picked up an American Music Award on behalf of the group from Dick Clark, he proceeded to thank Clark profusely but neglected to thank the DJs who had supported The Temptations throughout their career, and who promoted their new records. Street recalled:

> As soon as we heard his speech, we knew we were in trouble. The DJs blackballed us along with my lead song because they had not been given any recognition. 'Heavenly' and the follow-up Temptation song, 'You've Got My Soul On Fire', were no longer heard on the radio. They also blackballed other Motown acts that were on the charts at the same time. This hit Motown where it hurt the most, in the pocket!

This was a shame for both Street and the song itself, a beautiful ballad written by Whitfield, who could still produce a romantic number in the midst of all the heavy psychedelic tracks. Street sings the bulk of the verses, except for the lines 'I may not be the one you want/But I'm sure the one you need', which is sung by Harris and included in both verses. The backing vocals are a mix of 'sha-la-las' and call-and-response to Street, and are kept soft and sensual to counteract Street's pleading lead.

Yet, thanks to Abner's gaffe, fewer people heard the song than it deserved, although the group performed it on and off in concert over the next decade and it featured in Street's own shows once he left the group in the 1990s.

'You've Got My Soul On Fire' (Norman Whitfield)

More funky than 'I Need You', but still ostensibly a love song, Edwards sings the lead on 'You've Got My Soul On Fire', an intense ballad whose production masks some sweet, romantic lyrics. Once again, the bassline has an irresistible groove and is tightly locked together with the drums and Eddie 'Bongo' Brown's rhythmic playing. Whitfield layers this with both an acoustic guitar and Ragin's wah-wah guitar, along with organ, topped off with some forceful horns. Edwards sings the lead, while the rest of the group mirror his lead vocal in call-and-response style; the horns then punch in before the choruses bring in the drums and bass.

Lyrically, Whitfield wasn't that far from Marvin Gaye on his *Let's Get It On* album, with lines like: 'When you press your sweet lips to mine, oh baby/My blood starts boiling and my temperature starts to rise'. But unlike Gaye, Whitfield couldn't resist upping the tempo rather than having the group record it as a more traditional or sensual ballad. Such an intense, pounding track suits Edwards on lead perfectly – it's another powerful performance.

It was also the final single to be released from *1990*, and while it also reached number eight on the R&B charts, it could only reach number 74 on the pop charts. As Williams noted in his memoir, the group could still rely on their core audience to give them R&B hits, but sales were slipping overall.

'Ain't No Justice' (Norman Whitfield)

With the first four songs on *1990*, it seemed Whitfield had taken on board the criticism from Williams and the group, keeping them relatively short and to the point and largely away from heavier subject matters of life, death, poverty and politics. Yet, old habits die hard, and with 'Ain't No Justice', Whitfield returns to the long-playing message songs he'd perfected on *All Directions* and *Masterpiece*. The song explores the notion of American justice, or lack of, for minorities, asking the question, 'Why can't we live our lives and be friends?' In one section, Whitfield, somewhat prophetically of the current American political context, wrote:

There ain't no justice,
Build your walls,
Crawl into your holes,
Put out your signs,
Peep through your blinds
Call me, 'your kind'
I don't mind

Riser provides a suitably dark arrangement to accompany these philosophical lyrics, complete with eerie-sounding guitar, harsh synths, bluesy harmonica playing and a striking string section. The lead vocals are split between Street, Franklin and Harris.

Above: Atlantic Records promotional photograph of the new lineup of The Temptations. (*Atlantic*)

Left: The Temptations produced themselves on *Do The Temptations* (1976), their final album before leaving Motown. (*Gordy/Motown*)

Right: *Hear To Tempt You* (1977), the first album on Atlantic Records, introduced new lead singer Louis Price. (*Atlantic*)

Left: The second and final album for Atlantic, *Bare Back* (1978), was another disappointment for the group. (*Atlantic*)

The song then changes tempo around the three-minute mark, with Franklin boldly asking us to 'Close your eyes, I want you to take an imaginary trip with me', the 'me' swathed in echo, as the rest of the group take turns to sing 'Tomorrow' repeatedly. The sounds of children playing are mixed into the track, with initially just Jack Ashford's tambourine keeping the beat before the guitar re-enters the mix. For the final section, Edwards sings the lead in a higher octave than usual before Whitfield inserts a fiery guitar solo, something unusual for a Temptations record, and more suited to his other pet project, The Undisputed Truth. But as the wailing guitar ends, Edwards returns, this time back with his typical roar.

Again, Whitfield manages to cram a lot into 'Ain't No Justice', which runs to just over six minutes. Yet, unlike the 14-minute 'Masterpiece' or some of his other longer album cuts, it doesn't feel overly long or repetitive – another lost Whitfield masterpiece.

'1990' (Norman Whitfield)

The second side opens up with one of the boldest songs the group ever recorded, a damning indictment of America in the early 1970s. The song opens to the sound of an arrest of a black man, in which a white policeman uses the n-word while the arrest plays out; Edwards replies, to no avail, that 'this is supposed to be America, man'. Edwards continues with the lead, a natural choice given the powerful and damning lyrics, the first two verses pulling no punches:

> Well, we got trouble in the White House
> Poverty in the ghetto, yeah
> When will it end?
> Nobody knows!
>
> People are asking now
> 'How can you spend another dollar on the space race
> With families at home starving right in front of your face?'
> Where is your heart, America?

It's probably the most political song The Temptations ever recorded, and also one of their most underrated socially conscious songs. Whitfield keeps the song short, by his standards anyway, which adds to its impact; with the long, extended instrument breaks and solos now gone, it's much more in the mould of 'Ball Of Confusion' or 'War' than 'Masterpiece'. Given its incendiary lyrics, it's not that surprising Motown didn't release it as a single, but the song does end on a somewhat patriotic note, seemingly at odds with the rest of the song:

> Don't get me wrong, I still love ya,
> In spite of all your troubles and woes
> In my eyes you're still the greatest of them all!

It's a brilliant polemic on the state of America in 1973, after years of fighting in Vietnam, growing inner-city poverty and the ongoing Watergate saga. It covers similar themes to Gil Scott Heron's 'The Revolution Will Not Be Televised', but while Heron made no attempt to reconcile his take on America with the fabled American Dream, Whitfield had no such qualms. That might be in part due to his association with Motown, a true American success story, which, on this reading, could only have happened because of America's unique character and manifest destiny.

'Zoom' (Norman Whitfield)
Whitfield just couldn't help himself with 'Zoom': after trying his best to keep the rest of *1990* relatively short and to the point, he allows himself one final musical odyssey with The Temptations on the album's last track. Nearly 14 minutes in length, 'Zoom' is Whitfield's take on the US space programme, placing The Temptations on an imaginary trip to the moon.

Clearly taking inspiration from Gil Scott Heron again, whose own polemic 'Whitey On The Moon' reflected the feeling of many in the Black community that America might be better dealing with the problems on Earth rather than spending billions of dollars on spaceflights sending white men to the moon, Whitfield's lyrics are less incendiary, but the message is the same:

Everything in mind is higher
(Higher, higher, higher than ever before)
The crime rate is getting
(Higher, higher, higher than ever before)
My taxes are getting
(Higher, higher, higher than ever before)
All the people are getting
(Higher, higher, higher than ever before)
That building, building's
(Higher, higher, higher than ever before)
My music's gonna take you
(Higher, higher, higher than ever before)

This all happens by the six-minute mark, with the rest of the song a largely instrumental affair, with some guitar solos and an excellent trombone solo from George Bohannon, which seems to last forever. Not knowing when to stop, perhaps a take on the US government, Whitfield then has the group repeat the line:

The ride is out of sight
Taste of space
Zoom, zoom, zoom
Zoom, zoom, zoom

This seems to last an eternity, as Bohannon keeps playing his trombone, eventually coming to a close with the rest of the musicians falling back in. One of the more intriguing long-playing tracks from Whitfield, it was also the last song he produced for the group until they reunited nearly a decade later for a one-off reunion.

A Song For You (1975)

Personnel:
Otis Williams, Melvin Franklin, Dennis Edwards, Richard Street, Damon Harris: vocals
Donald Baldwin: clavinet, piano, saxophone, clarinet, Moog
Ollie E. Brown, Zachary Frazier, James Gadson: drums
Eddie Hazel, Melvin 'Wah Wah' Ragin: guitar
William 'Billy Bass' Nelson: bass
The Commodores: billed as 'The Temptations Band'
Produced at Motown Recording Studio, Hollywood, California, by Jeffrey Bowen, except 'Firefly' produced by James Carmichael and Suzee Ikeda, and 'I'm A Bachelor' produced by Terry Woodford and Clayton Ivery in 1974
Engineers: Cal Harris, Russ Terrana, Art Stuart, Fred Ross
Label: Gordy
Release date: 16 January 1975
Length: 37:53
Charts: US pop: 13, US R&B: 1

In an interview with *Soul Magazine* in 1977, just after The Temptations had left Motown, Williams described *A Song For You* as an album not good enough for 'a group of this calibre.' Perhaps his emotions were high given their acrimonious split from Motown, as he later wrote in his autobiography that it's 'my favourite record and one of our biggest commercial successes.' However, if the group were looking forward to an easier ride with a new producer after their split with the stubborn Norman Whitfield, they were in for a nasty surprise. Indeed, the recording of *A Song For You* was an incredibly tense affair.

The album paired the group once again with producer Jeffrey Bowen, who co-produced their album of standards *In A Mellow Mood* with Frank Wilson back in 1967. Unlike their previous effort, which Williams described as a 'pleasure' to record, this time, relations between the group and Bowen were strained to say the least. Williams described the recording sessions as 'some of the most miserable moments of my career', claiming that while Bowen was a fine producer, 'he cannot handle people, and before long, we started noticing a bad attitude on his part.' Eventually, things came to a head when Bowen lashed out at the group for failing to sing their parts as he wanted, and the group overheard him in the studio criticising their performance. Williams wrote that he wanted 'to kick Jeffrey's ass then and there, but the other guys in the group talked me out of it.' But even by the time he got home, Williams was so angry that he began shaking all over, and was hospitalised with stress. Berry Gordy tried to smooth things over, but understandably, the rest of the recording of *A Song For You* was strained.

If working with Bowen wasn't problematic enough, Damon Harris was beginning to drift away from the group, annoying Berry Gordy in one session with his lacklustre performance to the point that Gordy told Williams to fire him, the first time he had interfered in such a manner. And after one performance at the Apollo in Harlem, where Harris boasted to the audience how they'd made him and the others rich, the decision was taken to let him go. Williams reflected later that they were 'sorry to have to drop him, but, again, no one man is greater than the group.' Harris wasn't as polite, in an interview with *Blues & Soul* magazine, saying that the 'whole Motown experience left me pretty disillusioned and I couldn't accept the way the company functioned in certain respects. I couldn't deal with a lot of things that The Temps as a group were subjected to.'

Regardless of the tensions with Bowen and within the group, *A Song For You* would be the best Temptations album released during the second half of the 1970s: it has a coherent sound, the songs are mostly excellent and the vocals are impassioned.

Unlike *In A Mellow Mood*, this time around, Bowen brought the funk to The Temptations, clearly influenced by the new direction of funk by George Clinton and his Parliament-Funkadelic outfits. The A-side features some of the funkiest tracks that the group, and possibly Motown, ever recorded. This was in part thanks to the musicians Bowen tasked with creating the tracks, none other than The Commodores (billed as 'The Temptations Band' on the liner notes), who were on the cusp of stardom, thanks to their instrumental funk hit 'Machine Gun' released in 1974. Lionel Richie even gets a writing credit on 'Happy People'.

They were aided by additional musicians, including Funkadelic's Eddie Hazel on guitar (who had previously recorded a ten-minute guitar solo called 'Maggot Brain' for Funkadelic's album of the same name) and William 'Billy Bass' Nelson, also from Funkadelic. Funkadelic were part of George Clinton's 'P-Funk' empire, which emphasised psychedelic and rock sounds, whereas his other major group, Parliament, were a more polished and horn-driven funk outfit. Both sides of this 'P-Funk' influence are audible on *A Song For You* and give a harder edge than The Temptations' previous albums. Donald Baldwin, whom Bowen discovered while working at Holland-Dozier-Holland's Hot Wax and Invictus labels, also contributed several songs, along with Bowen, and played several of the instruments throughout. Meanwhile, the B-side is full of moody, emotional ballads, as was often the case with soul and R&B acts of the 1970s (one side for dancin', one for romancin').

Whereas recent albums with Whitfield had seen the lead vocals shared across the group more equally, Williams later accused Bowen of showing favouritism towards Dennis Edwards. Certainly, Edwards sings the majority of the lead on *A Song For You*, but the vocal arrangements are stunning, some of the best in the post-Classic Five era. Edwards does sing plenty of lead (and on 'Memories' it's essentially a Dennis Edwards solo song), but the other Temptations provide excellent backing vocals throughout, and share the leads on the album's funkier hits, in particular 'Glasshouse'.

A Song For You performed better than *1990*, hitting number one on the R&B charts, and peaking at number 13 on the US pop charts (although it didn't chart in the UK).

'Happy People' (Jeffrey Bowen, Donald Baldwin, Lionel Richie)
Initially penned in collaboration with Lionel Richie, 'Happy People' was originally intended for The Commodores before it was reallocated to The Temptations. It's simultaneously hard-hitting funk and proto-disco, with a blistering bassline, wah-wah guitars and a James Brown-esque horn arrangement. Bowen learnt the lessons of Whitfield's past efforts with the group, and the song is a radio-friendly three and a half minutes; if Whitfield had been given this song, it would no doubt have been a ten-minute funk odyssey.

Bowen produced a combination of Whitfield's brand of funk, with the even funkier P-Funk that George Clinton was pioneering. A new and exciting direction for The Temptations, yet they wouldn't recreate such funkiness again on any other album. It became a number-one hit on the US R&B charts, although it fared worse on the pop charts, stalling at number 40. It even reached number 11 on the new US disco charts, no doubt helped by its danceable groove.

'Glasshouse' (Charlemagne (TM) – James Carmichael, Ronald Miller, Kathy Wakefield)
The funk keeps rolling on *A Song For You* with 'Glasshouse', an immensely enjoyable track that has Edwards singing lead again, but with the other members chipping in with lines throughout. The song uses the idiom 'people who live in glass houses shouldn't throw stones' as its key message. It warns against hypocrisy, reminding listeners not to pass judgment when their own faults are exposed. The first verse makes it plain that we are all 'born alone' and we 'die alone', and between those two moments, we need to, essentially, mind our own business.

Perhaps one could read this as an attack on the ex-members of the group who criticise The Temptations in public. The second verse, though, suggests something else, a more liberal approach to sex, and possibly even same-sex relationships. Williams and Edwards share the following:

> I don't care
> What goes on in your house
> When you close the door
> If you stop lookin' in my bedroom window
> I'll stop lookin' in yours

Given the context of the time, six years after the Stonewall Riots in New York, where gay patrons of the Stonewall Inn protested against discrimination by the police and state, The Temptations could be making a political statement here. Alternatively, it might simply be another take on nosy neighbours and the dangers of gossip.

Either way, it's a phenomenally funky track and the vocal performances are equally powerful, helped, as usual, by Edwards's fiery delivery. Frustratingly for the group, when released as the third single from the album, it failed to match the success of 'Happy People', peaking at number nine on the R&B charts and number 37 on the pop charts.

'Shakey Ground' (Jeffrey Bowen, Eddie Hazel, Alphonso Boyd)
Co-written with Eddie Hazel, the incredibly gifted guitarist in Parliament-Funkadelic who wrote and performed the epic guitar solo on 'Maggot Brain', 'Shakey Ground' draws direct inspiration from the funky universes George Clinton's groups were creating in the 1970s, albeit in a softer, Motown-friendly way.

Edwards again sings the lead – Bowen clearly preferred his vocals to anyone else's in the group. His vocal is intense, reaching that shout-singing he mastered so well, while the backing vocals are mixed fairly low. The bass and guitar dominate the instrumentation with Billy 'Bass' Nelson, Funkadelic's original bass player, anchoring the groove, while Hazel handles the guitar parts. For good measure, there's a repetitive yet effective horn arrangement added. 'Shakey Ground' wouldn't sound out of place on any P-Funk record. It was released as the second single from *A Song For You*, hitting number one on the R&B chart and number 23 on the pop chart.

'The Prophet' (Jeffrey Bowen, Kathy Wakefield, Larry Duncan)
Inspired by the writings of Kahlil Gibran, whose best-known work was also called *The Prophet*, this was the one song on the album that Williams, in his memoir, claims he didn't like on *A Song For You*, writing, 'with all due respect to Kahil's fine work, the song just didn't cut it.' Gilbran's is split into 26 fables about a prophet who is dying in the city of Orphalese; knowing that he is dying, the local people seek the prophet's knowledge. The book deals with all elements of the human condition, the meaning of life and love. Bowen and his co-writers try to condense this into a song, dealing with these key themes.

The first verse sets the scene, beginning with a man and a woman crying out to the prophet to teach them about love and how to find it. The second verse, on which Franklin takes the lead, provides the prophet's response:

He said that love will call to you
So follow him, though it's hard to do
Believe, believe! We gotta believe!
Within your heart is the secret of life
With joy and sorrow, pleasure and strife
Love is all of these things

As in Gilbran's book, the lyrics show that love can be found everywhere and in anything. This is the case in the bridge, where we are told to 'work with love, and love your work' and that 'happiness sometimes hides in pain'. Compared with the rest of the album, it's a deeply philosophical track, somewhat reminiscent of Norman Whitfield's later productions on the group.

The arrangement itself is more cinematic than the rest of the album, with an Arabian feel thanks to the strings and horns. While the lead is split, Franklin speaks the last verses in his rumbling, deep voice. It's an ambitious track, but Williams is probably right to suggest it didn't quite fit with the rest of *A Song For You*.

'Happy People – Instrumental' (Jeffrey Bowen, Donald Baldwin, Lionel Richie)

The instrumental of 'Happy People' closes out the A-side, and is presumably included as simply 'filler' for the album in place of anything else decent enough to be included. The group are billed as 'The Temptations Band', but again, it's really the work of guitarists Eddie Hazel and Wah Wah Watson, and the incredibly heavy bass playing of Billy 'Bass' Nelson.

In his autobiography, Williams claims they had recorded another song, 'Soulmate', for the album, but it was rejected as not being strong enough. Presumably, this instrumental took its place here. It would, however, eventually be released on their *Emperors Of Soul* box set in 1994.

'A Song For You' (Leon Russell)

By the time The Temptations got around to recording 'A Song For You', it had already become one of Donny Hathaway's finest recordings, making the song his own. He wasn't the only artist to record it: Aretha Franklin recorded a predictably decent version on her album *Let Me In Your Life*, and even crooner Andy Williams had a minor hit with a version in 1971.

The Temptations' version, as might be expected, features an exceptional vocal arrangement. Edwards gives an impassioned lead vocal, and Franklin and Harris provide counterpoints between the bass and tenor vocals, especially as they repeat 'in a place, in a place' in a call-and-response with Edwards. This happens several times, for example:

> You came out in front when I was hiding (but you have nothing to hide)
> And now I'm so much better, and if my words, they don't come together
> Listen to the melodies (listen to the melodies)
> Cause my love, ooh baby, cause my love, cause my love, ooh
> Is in there, ooh, is in there hiding
> Baby I loved you in a place (in a place, in a place, in a place)
> Where there's no space or time
> (Baby I loved you) I loved you all my life

Unlike Hathaway's version, The Temptations' version seems somehow sadder, somewhat darker, perhaps the result of Edward's vocal or the brooding, moody instrumental track, complete with a mournful string arrangement. Edwards begins his lead almost whispering, far more restrained than usual, before building into his trademark growl, again, different from the smoother Hathaway. Yet, he ends the song on a softer note, proving that he, too, could be a romantic, in an era when smooth, soulful lover-men were coming to dominate.

'Memories' (Jeffrey Bowen, Donald Baldwin, Kathy Wakefield)
Bowen certainly had the knack for writing for Edwards, and along with collaborators Donald Baldwin and Kathy Wakefield, delivered another brooding ballad for him to sing. Edwards sings softly in the verses before building into his usual, almost shouting vocals in the choruses. The horns and strings are moody, while Baldwin's Moog playing gives the song an eerie, futuristic quality, again perhaps influenced by the intergalactic adventures of George Clinton. Yet, at times, the arrangement drowns out the relatively sparse backing vocals, something that irked the group.

'I'm A Bachelor' (Dennis Edwards, Otis Williams, David English, Richard Street, Damon Harris)
Written by the group themselves, its inclusion on *A Song For You* suggests it was more of a conciliatory attempt by Motown and Bowen, given the tensions in the recording sessions, rather than the quality of the song itself. With notable exceptions, there's a reason why Berry Gordy largely didn't want his artists writing their material: they could sing and perform, but that doesn't mean they can write.

That is a little harsh here, as 'I'm A Bachelor' isn't a bad song, but it's not the best on *A Song For You*. It's saved by its arrangement, which owes a lot to Norman Whitfield's brand of cinematic soul; it's dark and moody yet remains funky, anchored by Nelson's bass playing. Edwards sings the lead, but the harmonies are high up in the mix, particularly Franklin and Leonard, making for yet another great vocal performance.

'Firefly' (Jesse Boyce)
A softer ballad than the previous on *A Song For You*, 'I'm A Firefly' is a rare sharing of leads between Street and Franklin. It's a lovely moment between two old friends, with Street's tenor contrasting with the low rumbles of Franklin's bass. Franklin is also given a short spoken-word verse before Street takes back the spotlight, delivering what must surely rank as one of his best moments as a Temptation.

House Party (1975)

Personnel:
Otis Williams, Melvin Franklin, Dennis Edwards, Richard Street, Damon Harris, Glenn Leonard: vocals
The liner notes do not list the musicians used on this album
James Anthony Carmichael, Terry Woodford, Clayton Ivey, Ted Stovall, Harrison Calloway, Steve Cropper, Peggy Sandvig, H.B Barnum: arrangements
Produced at Motown Recording Studio, Hollywood, California, by James Anthony Carmichael, Suzee Ikeda, Steve Cropper, Bria Holland, Clayton Ivey, Terry Woodford, The Temptations between 1974 and 1975
Engineers: Lawrence T. Horn, Fred Ross
Remixing and mastering: Cal Harris
Label: Gordy
Release date: November 1975
Length: 34:38
Charts: US pop: 40, US R&B: 11

Following the success of *A Song For You*, Motown made the inexplicable decision to release *House Party,* a hodgepodge of unreleased tracks from the archive that Otis Williams described in his autobiography as 'a mismatched collection of, pardon my French, shit.'

Williams claims the album was assembled due to the unavailability of Jeffrey Bowen: they might not have liked working with him, but they could not deny the success of *A Song For You*, so it made sense for him to produce a follow-up. However, Bowen was not under contract at Motown, and they weren't willing to wait, so they instead looked to the archive for something to release. As a result, the album is not as strong as *A Song For You*, though it's not as bad as Williams claimed in his autobiography; that perhaps speaks more to Williams's anger at the album being released without his agreement or satisfaction. However, despite a respectable showing on the US R&B charts, it wasn't a major hit (if the album had been a hit, perhaps Williams might have changed his tune). Williams claimed that while they didn't necessarily want the album to perform poorly, its lack of commercial success didn't bother them hugely, either. Indeed, the group, according to Williams, 'were secretly hoping Motown had learned a lesson: the public expects The Temptations to uphold a certain level of quality.'

The album marked the appearance of Glenn Leonard as a Temptation, after the departure of Damon Harris. Leonard grew up in Washington, DC, and sang in a variety of groups, including The Chancellors and The Unifics, before forming True Reflection in 1973. The new group produced one decent album, titled *Where I'm Coming From,* on Atlantic Records, but a lack of promotion and fierce competition from other Philadelphia soul acts meant the album didn't make much impact. However, the album made an impression on Williams, who, looking to replace Damon Harris, sought him out, and

Leonard quit True Reflection to join The Temptations. He recalled in an interview with Kevin Goins, for the SoulMusic reissue of the *Hear To Tempt You* and *Bare Back* albums, that even while working with his own groups, 'my goal was to hopefully become a Temptation.'

As with later 1970s albums from the group, the songs do not match the quality of those recorded during the Whitfield era, but the vocal performances remain excellent. Edwards is at his impressive best, singing the bulk of the lead, but the others get in on the act, too – even Franklin and Williams get some lead to sing. Leonard also impresses, a fine singer who, unlike Damon Harris, didn't really sound like Eddie Kendricks and therefore added a different edge to the group's harmonies.

House Party features a variety of producers. It reunited the group with Brian Holland and Eddie Holland, back writing and producing projects for Motown, despite their acrimonious split from the label in 1967. The Holland duo went on to produce their 1978 album *Bare Back*. It also featured production from famed Stax Records guitarist, writer and producer Steve Cropper (who left the label in 1970 and eventually settled in Los Angeles), as well as James Anthony Carmichael and Motown fixer Suzee Ikeda. This mix of producers certainly didn't help the album sound as coherent as *A Song For You*.

'Keep Holding On' (Brian Holland, Eddie Holland)

The only single from the album, it reached a respectable number three on the US R&B charts and number 53 on the US pop charts, although it failed to break the UK singles chart. It's a funky opening combined with an intense disco beat, upon which Edwards lets rip on the lead vocal. The arrangement by James Anthony Carmichael is busy, and the backing vocals get a little lost in the mix, drowned out by some intense bass playing and a synth solo.

'It's Just A Matter of Time' (Frank Johnson)

The intensity continues on the album's second track, complete with another pounding bassline, with the addition of wah-wah guitar and a bold horn arrangement. Edwards again sings the lead, and given the intensity of the arrangement, it's likely the other Temptations struggled to keep up with the track and be heard over the instrumentation.

That said, the backing vocals are arranged better than 'Keep Holding On', with Franklin ad-libbing throughout, while the highs are impressively clear. The arrangement by Terry Woodford, Clayton Ivey, Ted Stovall and Harrison Calloway harks back to the earlier soundtracks to Blaxploitation films like *Shaft* and *Super Fly*, taking a cinematic approach, resulting in a sonically deeper song than the rest on *House Party*.

'You Can't Stop A Man In Love' (George Soule, Terry Woodford)

Originally recorded by Rueben Howell in 1973 for Motown, The Temptations' version here sounds a little dated compared to the rest of the album, suggesting it came from an earlier recording session. Edwards sings the lead once again, complemented by a lively backing vocal arrangement. Howell's original version has a Northern Soul flavour and is included in various Northern Soul compilation albums. Here, it's given a faster arrangement, influenced by both 'Philly Soul' and other disco tracks, but it doesn't hold up to the classics of either genre. Nor does it better the version recorded by Howell, whose yearning, bluesy arrangement suits the song much better.

'World Of You, Love And Music' (Steve Cropper, Artie Wayne)
The first of the Steve Cropper-produced songs, Edwards sings the lead once again. Cropper might have produced some of the finest songs at Stax, including Otis Redding's posthumous hit '(Sitting On) The Dock Of The Bay', but – if 'World Of You, Love And Music' is anything to go by – he lost his touch in the disco-dominated 1970s. The song itself is forgettable, despite the lush arrangement and the excellent vocal performances The Temptations deliver here, especially the ad-libbing in the middle of the song from Street and Williams. As with other songs in this period, their vocals aren't enough to overcome mediocre songwriting or producing.

'What You Need Most (I Do Best Of All)' (Dennis Edwards, David English, Damon Harris, Richard Street, Otis Williams)
Up until this point, it was rare for the group to record their own material; one of the biggest areas of conflict with Motown at this point was their lack of writing and producing on their own albums. The group had begun writing together, but the Motown management were unsure about giving them such artistic freedom. They had a point on 'What You Need Most (I Do Best Of All)': it's neither bad nor good, but it at least gave the group some experience writing and also some publishing royalties. In his autobiography, Williams claims he came up with the idea for the song, 'after being inspired by the sight of a woman I knew.'

Suzee Ikeda, a fixer at Motown who originally came to the label as a singer but ended up looking after a young Michael Jackson, among other things, produces the track. Sadly, it suffers a similar fate to others on *House Party* with a middling arrangement. Vocally, however, it's one of the more interesting songs on *House Party,* with the leads split between Street, Williams and new member Leonard. The songwriting is credited to former tenor Damon Harris, but Leonard excels in his old position in the group, sounding neither like Harris nor Kendricks. It's a shame for him that the song perhaps wasn't the best to kickstart his career as a Temptation.

'Ways Of A Grown Up Man' (Steve Cropper, Richard Cason, Billy Ray Charles)
One of the stronger moments on *House Party*, 'Ways Of A Grown Up Man' features a brilliant lead from Franklin, his voice reaching the lowest of his

range, making for one of the more unique leads in The Temptations' catalogue. Produced and arranged by Cropper along with H.B Barnum, this is a big improvement on 'World Of You, Love And Music'. The lyrics tell the story of a man leaving his rural home in the hope of a better life in the city. Franklin, as narrator, spends the song reassuring his mother of his decision to leave. Musically, the song has a danceable beat and funky bassline, complete with strings and horns that drive the song along, not dissimilar to the *1990*-era Whitfield productions. If only the rest of the album had followed this pattern.

'Johnny Porter' (Bobby Ray Appleberry, Bill Cuomo)
The last of the three Cropper-produced tracks features another lead by Edwards, who tells the story of Johnny Porter, a young man drawn into a life of crime, leaving his parents and victims in his wake as he goes on the run to avoid the inevitable. It's the sort of song that Edwards typically excelled on, and 'Johnny Porter' is no exception. The whole group sing the chorus, with Franklin doubling Edwards' lead in places. Cropper throws plenty of horns and strings into the mix to create an almost cinematic arrangement that builds in intensity as the song proceeds, and Johnny Porter begins his life on the run. The pace gets faster, and the horns and vocals become terser, giving the sense of danger and drama that someone on the run would experience. The song was later covered by the acapella group The Persuasions on their 1977 album *Chirpin'*.

'Darling, Stand By Me (Song For My Woman)' (Dennis Edwards, David English, Richard Street, Otis Williams)
Given Williams' dismissal of *House Party*, it features perhaps his finest lead as a Temptation, rare as those might be. Williams spent the majority of his time in the group in the background, at least vocally, being what Berry Gordy called the 'glue' of the group – anchoring the harmonies, while taking care of business for the group. As a result, Williams has few leads to his name, along with a few spoken-word monologues on songs like 'Masterpiece' or 'I'm Gonna Make You Love Me' with Diana Ross & The Supremes, although these spoken-word 'love notes' became more frequent in later decades. Yet, here, Williams gives a fine lead performance, backed by lush string and horn arrangements, plus some sweet backing vocal arrangements that feature Franklin and Leonard heavily. It also no doubt gave the group confidence in their writing abilities, having written and co-produced the song together.

'If I Don't Love You This Way' (Leon Ware, Pam Sawyer)
The album ends on another particularly strong song, the romantic 'If I Don't Love You This Way'. Richard Street is given the lead and does a great performance singing in a rougher and gruffer way than usual, even trying his hand at shouting several of the lines, following Edwards' playbook, although he's less successful than Edwards in this regard.

The song was written by Leon Ware and Pam Sawyer, who wrote the sensual 'If I Lose This Heaven' for Quincy Jones; Ware also brought his experience working with the king of seduction, Marvin Gaye, on his intensely sexual album *I Want You*. The song first appeared on The Jackson 5's *Dancing Machine* album in 1974, their penultimate release on Motown.

Here, however, Street delivers a better vocal than a pubescent Michael Jackson; these gorgeous mid-tempo ballads suited Street perfectly, and he would always excel on these when given the chance. The catchy chorus and the creative vocal arrangement support Street beautifully, making it the best song on *House Party*.

Wings Of Love (1976)

Personnel:
Otis Williams, Melvin Franklin, Dennis Edwards, Richard Street, Glenn Leonard: vocals
Truman Thomas, Sly Stone (uncredited): clavinet, organ and ARP synth
William 'Billy Bass' Nelson, Freddie Stewart: bass, guitar
Ollie E. Brown: drums, percussion
Rustee Allen: bass
Pat Rizzo, Steve Madiao: trumpets
Donald Baldwin: Moog programming, keyboards, rhythm and vocal arrangements
Truman Thomas: horn and string arrangements
Produced at Motown Recording Studio, Hollywood, by Jeffrey Bowen and Berry Gordy (executive producer) between 1975 and 1976
Recording and mastering engineer: Russ Terrana
Assistant engineers: Jack Andrews, Jane Clark
Mixing: Russ Terrana, Jeffrey Bowen
Label: Gordy
Release date: 10 March 1976
Length: 31:13
Charts: US R&B: 3, US pop: 29

If the group hoped to put the disappointment of *House Party* behind them, they wound up equally disappointed with the follow-up, *Wings Of Love*. Jeffrey Bowen was back producing the group, along with Berry Gordy, who served as executive producer. In reality, at least on Williams' account, it was Bowen who set the direction, and he seemed to have little interest in the group beyond having Dennis Edwards sing lead on all but one of the album's eight tracks, with Richard Street given the lead on 'China Doll'. Bowen then had the group's backing vocals mixed so low on the final tracks that the other Temptations would have been better off not recording anything. If you listen really carefully, you can just about hear the rest of the group, but it's hard to pick out the individual voices. In fact, according to author Mark Ribowsky, most of the vocals aren't The Temptations at all, as Bowen hired other singers to provide what little background vocals he included. These vocalists aren't credited on the album, but it's clear Bowen was only interested in Edwards singing the lead, all the time encouraging him to leave the group and go solo.

However, in its favour, the album is certainly funkier than *House Party* and sounds much more coherent. Several of the musicians Bowen used on *A Song For You* make a return, including William 'Billy Bass' Nelson from Funkadelic, as well as several members of Sly & The Family Stone, including both Sly himself and his brother Freddie. Sly's contributions went uncredited on the album, though, reportedly in an attempt to avoid the US Internal Revenue Service from taking money to cover his tax bill. The first side of the album is heavy on the funk, whereas side two, like *A Song For You*, is less for dancing but for romancing, featuring three decent ballads, all with Edwards on lead.

However, by this point, disco was dominating the charts, and *Wings Of Love* makes no attempt to embrace it, rightly or wrongly, and therefore sounds slightly out of touch compared with the hits of the year, such as Johnnie Taylor's 'Disco Lady' or Frankie Valli's 'December 1963'. Even James Brown was struggling to find an audience for his funk records, and in 1979, he ended up recording his own disco album, the modestly titled *The Original Disco Man*. Yet, even if Bowen had embraced disco for *Wings Of Love*, the songs on the first side of the album are largely forgettable, even with Edwards' incredibly powerful vocals.

Tensions between the group, in particular Williams and Bowen, reached new heights during the recording sessions. Williams made it clear to Berry Gordy that he wouldn't be working in such an environment again. Clearly, something needed to change for the group, and by this point, a departure from Motown was becoming a more attractive option. Glenn Leonard, who, unfortunately for him, joined at a rough time for the group, recalled that Motown had lost interest in the group, in part driven by the seemingly constant lineup changes. He told writer Kevin Goins:

> [T]here were so many changes within the lineup up to that point – it's David, Eddie, Paul and Damon leaving, while Richard, Dennis and I were coming in – that the interest in The Temptations, from the point of view of the fans and Motown, started to wane. The producers lost interest and we couldn't find a sound that would help carry us through.

This was not The Temptations of yesteryear and they were already being pigeonholed as an 'oldies' group, destined to tour the hits forevermore. As a result, only 'Up The Creek (Without A Paddle)' was released as a single, suggesting that even Motown knew *Wings Of Love* wasn't worth promoting, although according to Williams, Gordy actually liked the finished product, even though it sounded more like an Edwards solo effort rather than a proper Temptations album. Either Gordy was simply trying to placate the group or was alienated from current musical trends since he'd moved from Detroit to Los Angeles.

Despite all this, *Wings Of Love* sold better than *House Party*, reaching number three on the US R&B charts and number 29 on the pop charts, quite an achievement for a group struggling to find a sound.

'Sweet Gypsy Jane' (Jeffrey Bowen, Jimmy Ford, Truman Thomas)
The album opens with this slamming piece of funk, not dissimilar to The Temptations' earlier work with Norman Whitfield (or, for that matter, later Sly Stone material). Naturally, Edwards is given the lead vocal, and he's practically

shouting the verses: the material might have been weaker than before, but Edwards tried to overcome it with pure vocal firepower.

The arrangement is reminiscent of the funkier tracks on *A Song For You*, albeit with a more frantic pace. The instrumentation is loud and in-your-face, complete with screeching guitars and a fierce horn arrangement, anchored by William Nelson's pumping bass. Bowen then pans the guitar between the left and right channels, while the rest of the instrumentation pounds along relentlessly. However, as with most of the other songs on *Wings Of Love*, the rest of The Temptations feature low in the mix, essentially making this a Dennis Edwards solo song.

'Sweetness In The Dark' (Jeffrey Bowen, Truman Thomas)
Bowen keeps the funk coming, toning down the pace on 'Sweetness In The Dark' to create a mid-tempo ballad about a woman who 'turns my bed into a boat, rocks me to my soul'. The groove is infectious, but the largely repetitive lyrics let the song down: there are three short verses, but Edwards spends most of his time repeating the line 'Sweetness In The Dark' over and over. In the choruses, it's clear Bowen had Edwards double his vocal, harmonising with himself, but the rest of the group are nowhere to be heard.

'Up The Creek (Without A Paddle)' (Jeffrey Bowen, Jimmy Ford, Truman Thomas)
Three songs into *Wings Of Love* and, finally, the other Temptations are clearly heard. Naturally, Edwards takes the lead, but Leonard's tenor works to sweeten the arrangement, contrasting with the intensity of the instrumentation and the pounding slap-bass. Street is also allowed to ad-lib in the choruses, again, making this sound much more like a group effort than the rest of the album. It was also the only song to be released as a single from *Wings Of Love*, and it reached number 21 on the R&B chart, but could only peak at number 99 on the pop chart.

Sly Stone, a major inspiration for the group and Norman Whitfield in the 1960s, actually co-wrote 'Up The Creek'. Stone, by this point, had more or less abandoned his own career; key members of the Family Stone had joined bassist Larry Graham to create Graham Central Station, but he still had moments of magic left to give before he would eventually disappear from the music business completely.

'China Doll' (Jeffrey Bowen, Jimmy Ford, Truman Thomas)
This is the sole lead from Richard Street on *Wings Of Love*, and the only lead by a member other than Edwards. No doubt Bowen bowed to pressure from the rest of the group to share the leads more equally, but 'China Doll' does feel more like a token gesture than a serious attempt to record something decent. Street's vocal also sounds very quiet in the final mix, overpowered by the horns and the bass, which is surely a deliberate production decision.

Bowen wouldn't have done the same had Edwards been singing lead, but the song is less about Street's lead than the funk workout that Bowen had produced, complete with a drum breakdown. With stronger vocals, 'China Doll' could have been much improved.

'Mary Ann' (Jeffrey Bowen, Donald Baldwin, Jimmy Ford)
Side two of *Wings Of Love* changes direction, from blistering funk to an epic, seven-minute-long ballad about a woman called 'Mary Ann'. Edwards sings the lead, predictably, giving a dramatic lead vocal, and this time, Bowen includes the rest of the group, creating some dreamy backing harmonies to contrast with Edwards' gruff howls and screams.

Bowen then breaks the track down to just the electric piano halfway through the song before adding clavinet and synthesisers to add to the eerie, dramatic feel. Edwards reappears to sing the final verse, starting softly, eventually accompanied by the rest of the group harmonising on some elongated 'ahhhs'.

'Dream World (Wings Of Love)' (Jeffrey Bowen, Donald Baldwin, Jimmy Ford)
The dreamlike arrangements keep coming with 'Dream World (Wings Of Love)', with, you guessed it, Edwards on lead. Here, though, he's far more restrained, almost singing in a whisper, although by the mid-point of the song, as he reaches the chorus, he's back singing in his typically gruff way.

The song itself is better than 'Mary Ann', and the production is suitably sweet and romantic. The rest of the group, though, are largely singing the 'ooh's and 'ahh's before simply repeating the refrain 'You got me dreaming' as the song comes to a close, while Edwards vocalises and ad-libs over the top. These vocals sound good, but it's hardly the type of arrangement The Temptations were used to singing, nor had their fans come to expect. It's no wonder the other members felt disheartened when this was the bulk of their contribution to *Wings Of Love*.

'Paradise' (Jeffrey Bowen, Donald Baldwin, Jimmy Ford)
One of the better moments on the album, 'Paradise' is a soft ballad that demonstrates a softer, calmer side to Edwards that was rarely heard, compared with the rough toughness that usually characterised his singing. At times, he sounds uncomfortable at such a high vocal range, but this adds to the vulnerability of the song's narrator. Unfortunately, as with the rest of *Wings Of Love*, the rest of The Temptations barely feature on the track.

Do The Temptations (1976)

Personnel:
Otis Williams, Melvin Franklin, Dennis Edwards, Richard Street, Glenn Leonard: vocals
Melvin 'Wah Wah' Ragin: guitar
James Gadson: drums
Henry Davis: bass
Eddie 'Bongo' Brown: percussion
John 'Special Effects' Barnes: keyboards
Michael L. Smith, Benjamin Wright: arrangements
Produced by Tall 'T' Productions, Suzee Ikeda and Michael L. Smith in 1976
Engineers: Cal Harris, Art Stewart
Assistant engineer: Jane Clark
Mixing: Cal Harris
Label: Gordy
Release date: 16 August 1976
Length: 36:45
Charts: US Pop: 53, US R&B: 10

After *House Party* and *Wings Of Love*, relations between Motown and The Temptations had broken down. Disagreements about money naturally played a part – Otis Williams claimed that the group had missed out on $300,000 in royalty payments – but a perceived lack of respect and dignity towards the group was perhaps more important. The Temptations were no longer the naive teenagers they'd been when they'd first signed their contracts with Gordy and had naturally attempted to take greater control of their own business affairs. This, according to Williams, caused a wedge between the group and Motown, with their ingrained suspicion of outside managers and accountants.

They had already begun recording *The Temptations Do The Temptations* when the group's contract renewal came up. The album's premise was simple: The Temptations write and produce an album themselves for the first time. The group, in particular Williams, had been itching to have greater involvement in producing their records for years, and the failure of their last two albums seemed to vindicate their position. After all, other Motown acts had produced themselves to great success; The Temptations needed only to point to Stevie Wonder or Marvin Gaye, or even Smokey Robinson, to prove it could be done.

Presumably out of other ideas, and no doubt to fulfil their contractual obligations, Motown relented. They did, however, have Suzee Ikeda co-produce the songs, which were credited to 'Tall 'T' Productions': The Temptations themselves. Ikeda originally came to Motown as a singer and signed to their MoWest imprint in 1971, based in Los Angeles. But when her singing career ended, she stayed with the label, becoming an assistant to the likes of The Jackson 5 and The Commodores. Here, she performed a similar job for The Temptations.

Perhaps unsurprisingly, given that Dennis Edwards handled most of the leads on *Wings Of Love*, here the lead vocals are split more evenly, and there are some great vocal performances, in particular from Glenn Leonard. But perhaps Gordy was right to resist Williams and the group writing for themselves: with a few exceptions, the songs on *The Temptations Do The Temptations* aren't good enough for a group of The Temptations' stature. Not even the excellent vocal performances are enough to disguise the quality of the songs or production. They also appeared to have forgotten Gordy's early mantra: keep it simple, stupid. Instead, the group threw everything at the record: horns and strings galore make for some busy and cluttered tracks. The result is an album no better than *House Party* or *Wings Of Love*, which they disliked.

Indeed, these production choices led *The Temptations Do The Temptations* to suffer the same problem as their two previous albums in that it sounded dated in the era of disco. Yet, in his memoirs, Williams wrote that '*The Temptations Do The Temptations* remains one of our favourite albums, and it got some wonderful reviews.' Unfortunately, with the group about to defect to Atlantic Records, Motown – at least in Williams's version of events – 'had no incentive to promote the new album.' He went on to claim that 'we met lots of disk jockeys who told us that they loved the record and couldn't understand why Motown wasn't pushing it.'

But while Motown was no longer the musical force that it had been a decade earlier, it was still releasing excellent records. In 1976, it finally released the long-awaited epic from Stevie Wonder, *Songs In The Key Of Life*, and Marvin Gaye's sensual *I Want You*, two albums that sound remarkably fresh today. Sadly, the same can't be said for *The Temptations Do The Temptations,* lacking both the quality and vision of these classic albums. As Dennis Edwards later recalled in an interview with Jim Bailey, 'I think we did a good job, but it wasn't one of our best efforts. Sometimes, you need an outside critic to tell you what doesn't quite work.'

By this time, one can only assume that Motown's fabled weekly 'quality control' meetings had been cancelled, or Motown just wanted one last product out on The Temptations before they, too, jumped ship. One thing that cannot be faulted here is the quality of the vocal performances: the harmonies from this lineup rival those of any Temptations era.

'Why Can't You And Me Get To Together' (Benjamin Wright, David English, Glenn Leonard, Otis Williams, Richard Street)

The album opens with a pleasant attempt at Philadelphia Soul, with a big horn and string arrangement combined with some tight harmonies. The arrangement is certainly smooth, but the lyrics are a little saccharine to say the least. The song tells the story of a man determined to impress his crush by playing tennis, even if he doesn't know how. The group sing some less-than-impressive lyrics, with verses like:

> Tennis court, I don't know the sport
> The game I came to play is of a different sort
> But if I have to play to get next to you
> I brought a racket and two brand new tennis shoes

It's a long way from the gritty social commentary of the early 1970s, or the often simple yet charming Smokey Robinson-penned ballads of the 1960s, perhaps reflecting their own newfound middle-class status. It's unlikely they'd have played tennis to impress a lady in Detroit, but since Motown moved to Los Angeles, maybe they'd gone soft. But, if anything, this song justifies Motown's reluctance to let the group write for themselves.

'Who Are You (And What Are You Doing With The Rest Of Your Life)' (Benjamin Wright, David English, Glenn Leonard, Otis Williams)
The light disco continues with 'Who Are You', which doesn't suffer to the same degree as 'Why Can't You' in terms of its lyrical content, but it's still not particularly inspiring or memorable. The song bounces along, complete with another big string orchestration and horn arrangement. The bass, played by Henry Davis, drives the song forward; he pops the strings with vigour, and his bassline is prominent in the final mix. Around the three-minute mark, there's a breakdown in which John 'Special Effects' Barnes provides a synthesiser solo, which sounds a little out of place when contrasted with the strings.

Similar to the album's first song, everything is thrown into the mix, and when it all comes together, it's a little overwhelming. Edwards sings the lead, while the group's harmonies surround him with plenty of energy, and as the song ends there's some ad-libs and vocalising from Edwards and Leonard. The song might be average, but the vocals can't be faulted.

'I'm On Fire (Body Song)' (Benjamin Wright, David English, Glenn Leonard, Otis Williams, Richard Street)
One of the standout moments on *Do The Temptations*, and one of Leonard's best leads, 'I'm On Fire' was a rare moment where the group, with the help of longtime collaborator Benjamin Wright, were able to craft something truly incredible. The song is a slow, super-romantic ballad which doesn't suffer the fate of the album's first two songs; instead, it's lightly orchestrated, with a more nuanced arrangement that allows the group to showcase their vocals without being overwhelmed. Indeed, it's Leonard's vocals that make the track: he delivers a phenomenal lead, reaching the peak of his range without sounding strained or forced. The other Temptations once again deliver some excellent backing vocals, with Street also reaching the highest of his vocal range, echoing Leonard in parts, with Franklin doing the same. As the song

reaches its climax, Leonard holds his note for an impressive 20 seconds as the song fades out, which makes purchasing the album worth it.

'Put Your Trust In Me Baby' (David English, Glenn Leonard, Otis Williams)

Sadly, after the respite of 'I'm On Fire', the album picks up where 'Who Are You' left off with the complex, orchestrated arrangements. The song opens with Franklin vocalising his trademark 'boom-booms'. It has yet another light disco arrangement: predictably, there are more strings and horns, but there are finger-snaps as well and a little wah-wah guitar in the introduction.

There are also more synths, no doubt from John 'Special Effects' Barnes, although these sound like they were taken from the soundtrack to an early computer game. They don't suit the rest of the smooth, melodic arrangement. Compared with other songs from the same year, such as Stevie Wonder's *Songs In The Key Of Life*, the synths sound basic and unnecessary.

Leonard sings the bulk of the lead before Edwards takes over forcefully as the song reaches its climax, ad-libbing and yelling at the woman in question to put her trust in him – possibly not the most reassuring approach to take when it comes to trust.

'There's No Stopping (Till We Set The Whole World Rockin')' (Michael Larry Smith)

The light disco turns into some sort of funk disco with 'There's No Stopping'. The bass is heavy and pounding, the horns are extremely loud and there's plenty of guitar soloing, too. Given the intensity of the track, it's no surprise that Edwards is given the lead, being the only one who could navigate the track's force. Street and Franklin are thrown a couple of lines to sing, but Street in particular sounds lost in the mix, unable to keep up with the pace of the track. Clearly aimed at the disco market, it features a frantic drum track along with a percussive breakdown about three-quarters into the track, with former Funk Brother Eddie 'Bongo' Brown living up to his nickname. There's also a guitar solo that precedes Brown; this is unusual for a disco track as, usually, the guitars are given a more rhythmic, percussive role.

Lyrically, the song takes inspiration from The O'Jays' 'Love Train', inviting anyone from anywhere to join The Temptations' party, no matter race or gender. But, unlike 'Love Train', this is an intense and exhausting listen, sounding almost like a workout, in which Dennis Edwards joins you in the gym and shouts at you to move quicker.

'Let Me Count The Ways (I Love You)' (David English, Dennis Edwards, Glenn Leonard, Otis Williams, Richard Street)

Thankfully, after the intensity of the last song, the group slow things down with 'Let Me Count The Ways', which features nearly all members of The Temptations on lead. Franklin opens up the song with a mix of spoken-word and singing before the group begin a countdown of why the lady in the song is so special. Each Temptation, minus Edwards – surely a deliberate choice after his dominance on *Wings Of Love* – sings a line after the countdown, with Street singing a verse later on. He strains to reach the high notes, but then allows his voice to soften beautifully as he comes out of holding the high note, returning the song to Franklin, who sings the same line repeatedly. The vocal arrangement is creative, especially with the countdown, helping to make some very soppy lyrics ('when you talk, you sound so sexy') bearable.

'Is There Anybody Else' (Benjamin Wright, David English, Glenn Leonard, Otis Williams, Richard Street)
A mid-tempo breakup song, 'Is There Anybody Else' tells the story of a man who suspects his woman is cheating, fearing that their love is 'slipping away'. It opens with just bass, drums and guitar licks before the strings swoop in and drive the song forward. Leonard sings the bulk of the lead, along with bright harmonies. Sadly, the song itself is rather pedestrian, lacking the bite that a breakup song should have; the sweet and romantic music contrasts with the sad lyric, but unlike the classic Motown hits that employ this tactic, it's largely forgettable filler.

'I'll Take You In' (Michael L. Smith)
The only song on the album not written by The Temptations but by Michael L. Smith, it's a typical ballad where a guy picks up the pieces after another guy breaks his crush's heart. Edwards sings the lead and starts rather mellow, but he quickly reaches boiling point, near shouting, as he tells the woman that he'll take her in. Again, like on 'Put Your Trust In Me Baby', it's perhaps not the best way to ask someone out, but his emotional power can't be denied. The rest of The Temptations keep up with Edwards, mirroring his vocals in a way not dissimilar to the way the Pips backed Gladys Knight, echoing and answering Edwards' lines. The song builds towards a final breakdown in which Edwards returns to a softer vocal, backed by just drums, bass and organ, before the rest of the group join in.

It's one of the better-produced tracks on *Do The Temptations,* and a decent way to finish a rather disappointing album.

Here To Tempt You (1977)

Personnel:
Otis Williams, Melvin Franklin, Richard Street, Glenn Leonard, Louis Price: vocals
Norman Harris, Bobby Eli, T.J. Tindal: guitars
T.G. Conway, Ron Kersey, Bruce Gray, Cotton Kent: keyboards
Richard Adderley: vibes
Ron Baker, Michael Foreman: bass
Keith Benson, Earl Young: drums
Larry Washington: congas
Don Renaldo and his string and horn section
Produced at Atlantic Studios, New York, and Sigma Sound Studios, Philadelphia, by Norman Harris and Ron Baker in 1977
Executive producer: Tall 'T' Productions
Engineer: Bobby Warner, Carl Paruolo, Dick Devlin
Label: Atlantic
Release date: 10 November 1977
Length: 40:07
Charts: US Pop: 113, US R&B: 38

After the disappointments of *Wings Of Love* and *Do The Temptations*, the group left Motown in the hope of finding greater success at Atlantic Records. The split was less than amicable, and the group trashed Motown in an interview in *SOUL*, claiming a lack of promotion, decent material and sympathetic producers. It didn't help either that Dennis Edwards sang almost all of the lead on *Wings Of Love*, causing the others to feel left out. Given the animosity, it was perhaps no surprise that Edwards did not join them at Atlantic.

In an interview with Leonard Pitts, provocatively titled 'Dennis Edwards and The Sinking Of The Good Ship Temptations', Edwards claimed The Temptations had gone from being 'the baddest group in the world' to one living purely on past glories. He accused Otis Williams and Melvin Franklin of refusing to change with the times, citing the success of The O'Jays and Gladys Knight & The Pips as prime examples of groups who'd changed their style and sound to achieve greater success. He clearly felt mistreated by the group, especially after he had helped them overcome the departure of David Ruffin. But he had clearly reached the end (at least for now) with how the group was running, saying that while, in theory, each member had one vote on group decisions, it was clear who had the final say:

> I was a replacement ... You're always reminded of that, and it's their right to remind you. People have accepted me before my group did. The fans have been great.

Keen not to burn all his bridges – wisely, given that he would return to the group in 1980 – he ended the interview on a conciliatory note:

> I wish 'em all the luck in the world ... I just hope they become the number-one group again. If they do, I'll find out maybe I was the problem.

Edwards might have had his run-ins with the other Temptations, but their issues ran deeper than just him, as their time at Atlantic Records would prove shortly. For Edwards, though, that probably wouldn't have been much comfort at the time: despite recording several tracks, Motown failed to release a solo album with him, and he ended up working for his uncle on a construction site in Cleveland.

Meanwhile, continuing with their motto that 'no man is greater than the group', The Temptations wasted little time in hiring a replacement, the 24-year-old Louis Price. He had been recommended to them by Fred Gooden and Sam Cash of The Impressions, who initially auditioned him to join their group. Given that Price would be following in the footsteps of both Edwards and David Ruffin, the group sounded bullish about their new label and lineup. Williams told *SOUL*, somewhat defensively:

> I think the public is waiting for us to come out with a fellow that sounds like Dennis. Louis don't sound nothing like Dennis. He don't sound nothing like David. Louis sounds like Louis Price.

The group, at least publicly, seemed reinvigorated with the new lineup and the new label. In another interview, with *Jet Magazine*, Melvin Franklin was slightly more cautious, saying the group were 'frightened' after leaving Motown, but that 'if we didn't think it was the right move, we wouldn't do it.'

The deal may have made financial sense, helped by the promise of better material, promotion and creative freedom, but by 1977, Atlantic Records was no longer the pioneering force in soul music it had been in the 1950s and 1960s. It had already pivoted to signing rock artists, such as Led Zeppelin, but it did have success in disco, and it couldn't ignore the huge success of 'Philly Soul' either, with Philadelphia International Records (PIR) essentially replacing Motown as the key driving force of popular black music in the 1970s. Therefore, it seemed sensible to reposition The Temptations' sound to take advantage of this new approach to R&B. As Leonard recalled in an interview with Kevin Goins, Atlantic originally sought out Kenny Gamble and Leon Huff, the PIR founders, to produce the record, but declined due to their own commitments with their own roster of acts. Instead, Atlantic turned to Norman Harris, Ronnie Baker and Earl Young.

The trio had an impressive track record in early disco at Philadelphia International Records with MFSB and The Trammps, with the latter's drummer Earl Young being credited with pioneering the 'four-on-the-floor' disco beat. However, by 1977, disco had evolved: more electronic sounds were emerging from the likes of Giorgio Moroder, while Nile Rodgers and Bernard Edwards were creating a new minimalist disco sound with Chic, Sister Sledge and eventually Diana Ross. Harris, Baker and Young, however, didn't seem to get the memo, sticking to the large orchestrations of earlier PIR records and sticking The Temptations on top.

As on *The Temptations Do The Temptations*, the songs on *Hear To Tempt You* just aren't good enough to rescue the album from the dated sound. Indeed, it's hard to believe Chic would release 'Everybody Dance' the same year that Atlantic put out *Hear To Tempt You*. Plus, while Louis Price could certainly sing, his voice was perhaps too different to what had gone before. He had a big job to replace the man who so ably replaced David Ruffin. In his memoirs, Williams wrote that Harris' production of 'strong percussion and swoop strings with Louis's smooth, mellow-sounding voice resulted in an odd mix.' However, given the arrangements, even Dennis Edwards would likely have struggled.

If The Temptations were hoping for a more collaborative effort compared with their later albums at Motown, they were to be disappointed: most of the productions were complete by the time the group heard them, and simply needed their vocals added. Harris and Baker had already recorded the tracks at Sigma Studios in Philadelphia and recorded the vocals in New York. Leonard recalled that 'I felt we didn't really connect with the music ... It looked as if the songs were created in a rush rather than tailor-made for us.'

As a result, *Hear To Tempt You*, ironically, didn't tempt many buyers: it only reached number 113 on the *Billboard* albums chart, and just number 38 on the R&B albums chart. Yet, while the album might have been a disappointment for a group looking for a new start, it did introduce them to a young singer-songwriter named Ron Tyson, who would eventually join the group in 1983 and would prove himself to be a devoted member.

'Think For Yourself' (Allan Felder, Norman Harris, Ron Tyson)

The album opens with a big classic-sounding, disco-oriented track, with intense swooping strings, a four-on-the-floor drum pattern and a frantic bassline. The song sounds very similar to the types of song recorded by the disco group The Trammps, with whom Harris, Baker and Young recorded earlier in the 1970s. The Trammps were a quintessential disco band: their songs featured the classic four-on-the-floor beat, funky basslines, horns that punched and strings that added energy and drama. 'Disco Inferno' is the best example, with its relentless beat, swirling strings and powerful lead vocal from singer Jimmy Ellis.

Yet, with Louis Price as the new Temptation, the group lacked a powerful lead singer like Ruffin or Edwards to attack this disco-oriented track. Price was not a gospel-shouter like Edwards nor as rough or as passionate as Ruffin. Instead, his voice was far smoother and softer, resulting in a more polished vocal performance that's less gritty and raw.

The song itself begins as a defence of the US president – peanut-farmer turned politician Jimmy Carter – with Price singing 'We're expecting miracles from the White House, tell me how much can one man do?' Not, perhaps, the campaign slogan Carter would have wanted for his doomed re-election campaign, but the sentiment of the song reflects the James Brown school of Black capitalism and self-sufficiency: it's up to you to sort your lives out, not anyone else's, so 'stop depending on someone else, do your job, think for yourself'. The lyrics are somewhat catchy, though they lose their punch being swathed in strings and horns. With better, more tailored arrangements, Price would have made a fine lead singer, but Harris and Baker decided to plough on with their brand of disco regardless of the singers in front of them.

'In A Lifetime' (Ron Baker, Ron Tyson)
The pounding, unrelenting drums continue on 'In A Lifetime', a song which is part disco-floor filler and part break-up ballad, in which the narrator – Leonard is on the lead here – simply won't find a love like the one he's lost in a lifetime. Harris and Baker employ the classic Motown approach of disguising the sadness of the song's story with an uptempo, danceable beat. They also have the group sing the line 'I'll never find another love like yours/In a lifetime, in a lifetime' repeatedly, and it becomes tiresome quickly. Indeed, the song is repetitive overall, not helped by the four-on-the-floor disco drum pattern which dominates the mix. The rest of the instrumentation sits behind the drums and the bass, while strings and horns are layered over the top.

'Can We Come And Share In Love' (T. G. Conway, Bruce Gray)
Price takes his second lead on *Hear To Tempt You* on the ballad 'Can We Come And Share In Love', and his voice sounds more natural on this slower number than on the frantically paced 'Think For Yourself'. His silky baritone is refreshing, different to the raspy grit of Ruffin and Edwards, but here he delivers the standout moment of his short tenure with the group.

The song's narrator is trying to convince a woman he fancies to share in his love; this being the 1970s, there's reference to the incompatibility of their star-signs (on their 1974 album *In Japan!*, The Temptations introduce themselves with their star-signs), but as Price sings, 'each time you touch me/I know that we're an exception to the rule'.

These slightly clunky lyrics aside, 'Can We Come And Share In Love' is one of the better moments on *Hear To Tempt You*. The orchestra is arranged with greater restraint than on the first two tracks; their lines are smoother and softer, resulting in an overall intimate mood.

'She's All I Got' (Ron Baker, Ron Tyson)
After that romantic interlude, the big disco numbers make a return with another Baker-Tyson composition. The song opens with a keyboard solo before the disco-drumming comes crashing back in. There's a thumping bassline, too, that overpowers the other instruments; the keyboards are mixed quietly, and if there are any guitars on the track, they're barely audible.

Price sings the lead again, and he does better than on 'Think For Yourself' at keeping up with the arrangement. Sadly, though, Baker and Tyson's lyrics are predictable and rely on conventional cliches to describe the woman in question:

> I need her sweet inspiration morning, noon and night (Sweet, sweet, so sweet)
> I've got so much respect for my lady
> Anything she says is right, hey-yeah
> Making love to her is so darn good
> It gets better every time
> And I'm so glad that she's with me
> 'Cause a good woman's hard to find

'Snake In The Grass' (T.G. Conway, Allan Felder, Ron Tyson)
The unrelenting disco sound continues, this time on 'Snake In The Grass', on which Street is given his first lead on the album, and although he, too, has a more mellow, smooth voice, it works a little better, perhaps because he was more confident and had more experience than Price in his abilities as a Temptation. Street also attempts to be gruffer, almost shouting in some of the verses, doing his best Dennis Edwards impression. The song opens with a short 20-second cinematic introduction made up of just hi-hat and repeated chords on the piano, along with a little wah-wah guitar and a slow, rising horn line that gives the sense something is looming. What is looming, though, is another unrelenting, pounding disco beat, with plenty of horns and strings thrown into the mix. There's a brief respite around the three-minute mark with a breakdown (common on disco tracks), which leaves Street vocalising with the drums and piano for a few seconds, before the horns and return.

It's not a bad effort, although the lyrics themselves are a little clichéd, and as good as Street is, he, too, lacks the vocal strength to pull disco off convincingly. As a genre, disco might have been formulaic (at least when done badly), but the vocals were usually big, bold and brash – even Victor Willis's vocals on the Village People's records were powerfully gruff. With this lineup of Temptations, though, that vocal firepower was diminished, resulting in tracks like this.

'It's Time For Love' (Allan Felder, Norman Harris, Ron Tyson)
Another big Philly soul, disco-oriented number, 'It's Time For Love' is not a ballad as such, but a plea for man (and woman) to love one another, so that they can all live in harmony. Important philosophical stuff, no doubt, and while certainly many Philadelphia soul tracks covered similar themes, Kenny Gamble and Leon Huff practically perfected a formula for message songs. However, their protégées, at least here, were unable to match their standards, and the result on this track is less impressive. The lyrics feel naive and more

contrived, especially lines like 'We've got to love our enemies, like they're our brothers', and Price's voice, impressive as it is, simply doesn't suit these big disco productions.

'Let's Live In Peace' (Melvin Franklin, Glenn Leonard, Louis Price, Richard Street, Otis Williams, Benjamin Wright)
Given the group's desire to write and produce themselves, which was in part a reason for their departure from Motown, they contribute just one song on *Hear To Tempt You*, the utopian 'Let's Live In Peace', written in collaboration with Benjamin Wright. A noble theme for a song, no doubt, but here it suffers a similar fate to 'It's Time For Love', sounding a little forced and contrived.

The arrangement at least is better; the slow groove suits Price better, and as a result, he sounds more comfortable, more impressive, even if the lyrics aren't great. The backing vocals, meanwhile, are excellent, with Leonard's soft tenor dominating in the mix, proving that, once again, even if the material was sub-par, The Temptations could still impress vocally.

'Read Between The Lines' (T.G. Conway, Allan Felder, Ron Tyson)
After a brief respite from the big disco arrangements, 'Read Between The Lines' returns the group to the discotheque, this time with a rare lead from Williams. Yet, like Price, he suffers from both the material itself and the arrangement. Williams is at his most impressive on ballads or mid-tempo grooves like 'Darling, Stand By Me' from *House Party*. His voice simply doesn't suit disco or fast-paced tracks.

He tries his best and delivers a surprisingly powerful performance, but he sounds like he's struggling to keep up with the frantic four-on-the-floor disco beat. Leonard steps in to handle the high notes and is able to navigate the arrangement better, but it's not enough to save the song.

'I Could Never Stop Loving You' (Allan Felder, Norman Harris, and Ron Tyson)
Hear To Tempt You ends with a rare lead from Franklin on this decent ballad, which, while still firmly disco-oriented, is much more enjoyable than the rest of the album. It's probably the best song on it: a pleasant, if generic, ballad in which Franklin, as narrator, just can't get enough of his woman's love. It's simple, uncomplicated, and as a result, it's more satisfying than the rest of *Hear To Tempt You*. Unsurprisingly, it features another lush-sounding orchestral backing, but it's not overpowering and, given the slower pace of the song, Franklin is able to navigate the arrangement well, sounding more comfortable than Price or Williams on earlier tracks.

Bare Back (1978)

Personnel:
Otis Williams, Melvin Franklin, Richard Street, Glenn Leonard, Louis Price: vocals
Ben Adkins, Tony Newton: bass
Quentin Dennard: drums
Tim May, Ben Benay, Wali Ali: guitars
Ronnie Coleman: electric piano
Sylvester Rivers: acoustic piano
Eddie 'Bongo' Brown, Bob Zimmitti: percussion
Michael Boddicker: synthesiser
George Bohanon, M. Creary, Stafford Floyd: trombone
Rodney J. Brown, Oscar Brashear, Walter Johnson: trumpet
Ernest Watts, William Green, Terry Harrington, John Hargrove: woodwinds
Vincent DeRosa, Arthur Maebe, Barbara Konn, Sidney Muldrow, Marilyn Robinson: French horn
Harry Bluestone: strings concert master
McKinley Jackson: rhythm arrangements
Paul Riser: horn and string arrangements
Produced at Wally Heideer Studio #4, Los Angeles; Kendun Recorders, Burbank; Studio Masters, Burbank, by Brian Holland
Executive producers: Eddie Holland, Tall T Productions
Engineers: Barney Perkins, Don Blake
Assistant engineer: Joe Laux
Mastering: Artisan Sound Recorders, Los Angeles
Label: Atlantic
Release date: 20 September 1978
Length: 34:58
Charts: US R&B: 46

After the relatively mediocre showing of *Hear To Tempt You*, Atlantic decided to pair The Temptations with fellow ex-Motown colleagues Brian and Eddie Holland for the follow-up, *Bare Back*. In the 1960s, their work with Lamont Dozier (known as Holland-Dozier-Holland, or simply 'H-D-H') resulted in some of Motown's finest ever recordings, giving hits to the likes of The Supremes and Four Tops.

With their acrimonious split from Motown in 1968, they struck out on their own with their Invictus and Hot Wax labels, creating hits for the likes of Chairmen of the Board and Freda Payne. But by 1978, their best work was long behind them: music had moved on, disco was triumphant, and the Holland brothers didn't seem to know what to do. They also brought in longtime collaborators Paul Riser and McKinley Jackson to write the arrangements, but even they struggled with the lacklustre material the Holland brothers had to offer.

In an interview with Kevin Goins, Glenn Leonard claimed that it was Atlantic who brought in the Hollands, and that the group supported the decision to work with their old friends:

> We went with the Hollands because they were familiar with The Temptations. They were used to our sound and vice versa.

Indeed, the Hollands had contributed a few songs to earlier albums by The Temptations. Notably, Eddie Holland in particular had co-written with Norman Whitfield on 'The Girl's Alright With Me' and 'Girl (Why You Want To Make Me Blue)'. These featured Eddie Kendricks on lead, and by the time the Hollands got their chance to produce a full Temptations album, of course, they were not the same group. However, as Leonard recalled, the Holland Brothers were keen to try 'something edgy', and the result was the song 'Bare Back'.

Compared with *Hear To Tempt You*, the leads are shared around more on *Bare Back*, with Richard Street and Glenn Leonard in particular benefiting. Leonard's leads are the best the album has to offer, rescuing it from being completely forgettable, particularly on the ballads 'Ever Ready Love' and 'Wake Up To Me'. Louis Price, meanwhile, nominally the group's lead singer, doesn't get as much airtime. Perhaps the Hollands were used to working with the likes of David Ruffin or Levi Stubbs of Four Tops – powerful gospel singers – or maybe they were simply trying something new for the group.

Either way, the Hollands could not improve the situation for The Temptations. According to Williams, writing in his memoirs, the album 'sounded hot enough, and the tunes were all solid, but while it did better than the previous record, it couldn't compete on the disco-dominated charts.' Yet, Williams' recollection is contrasted by the album's chart performance: it only reached number 46 on the R&B charts, and it failed to reach the pop charts at all. Even *Hear To Tempt You* made it to number 113 on the pop charts, although by previous standards, this, too, was a dismal performance. As a result, this ended up being the last Temptations album Atlantic released.

'Mystic Woman (Love Me Over)' (Richard Davis, Brian Holland, Eddie Holland)

The album opens with a funk-meets-disco workout, with the lead vocals split between Leonard and Street, setting the pattern for the majority of the album. The arrangement is much more invigorating than anything on *Hear To Tempt You*; Paul Riser's horn section in particular is plenty funky, creating a fierce groove.

The lyrics, however, let the song down somewhat. Leonard and Street sing about chasing a 'mystic woman' who they want to 'love me all over'; indeed, their potential love together with this 'twentieth-century girl' could be so powerful as to bring about 'new horizons'. There's also a reference to the film *Star Wars*, which came out the year before, in the first verse:

Live inside your force
Steady on your course
Let me trip into your star war world

Maybe the Hollands were simply fans of the film, or maybe they were trying to join the *Star Wars* bandwagon. Thankfully, the vocals from The Temptations are more inspired than the lyrics, with Street and Leonard's blend of vocals matching the energy of the song's arrangement.

'I Just Don't Know How To Let You Go' (Brian Holland, Eddie Holland, Marcia Woods)
The last single to be released from *Bare Back*, with the B-side 'Mystic Woman', is another jam that is both funky and disco-tinted. The lead begins with Street before handing over to Louis Price, who sounds more comfortable as a Temptation, although, like on *Hear To Tempt You*, his voice doesn't necessarily suit the disco-oriented sound the Hollands were unsuccessfully pursuing. Lyrically, the song compares love to a roller coaster and a 'rocky boat' that's 'out of gas' – hardly the same lyrical excellence the Hollands delivered at Motown.

The production is similar to 'Mystic Woman', with the Hollands throwing everything at the track: strings, horns, a pumping bassline and synths. All combine to create a dramatic, almost cinematic effect. Not that it helped: when it was released as the final single in March 1979, it flopped, failing to chart on either the R&B or pop charts. There was simply better disco material out there, and promotion was minimal, as, by this point, it was clear there would be no future for The Temptations at Atlantic.

'That's When You Need Love' (Richard Davis, Brian Holland, Eddie Holland)
After two dance numbers, the Hollands slow the tempo down a notch with 'That's When You Need Love', a mid-tempo stepper that has Price on lead, the only solo lead he's given on *Bare Back*. There's another large dose of disco here, notably the lush strings and the slightly more muted horn section, along with another pounding bassline. Price does his best, however, and it's possibly his best performance on record during his short time with the group; he sounds more controlled and assertive as a Temptation, though he lacks the power of Dennis Edwards. Unfair comparisons aside, it's one of the better tracks on *Bare Back*.

'Bare Back' (Harold Beatty, Brian Holland, Eddie Holland)
Ostensibly about making the most of life and avoiding complications and confrontations, it's hard not to overlook the sexual nature of the term 'bare back'. In his interview for the reissue of the album, Leonard claims that when presented with the song, the group were a little shocked to say the least, it being unlike anything they'd recorded so far. The Hollands told Street simply to 'have a little fun with it' when recording his vocals.

Street makes no mention of this song in his memoirs, and he sings the lyrics in a straightforward fashion, giving no indication about what he's actually saying, even when he sings:

Ride it bare back
Get up on it and ride
Ride it bare back
It's the natural thing to do

Despite the suggestiveness of the lyrics, the delivery by The Temptations is straight, even if the album cover features the group topless with their literal bare backs photographed. Yet, when interviewed for the CD reissue later on, Leonard recalled that it was the Hollands' intention to do something that 'had shock value, to get people's attention … You know the old saying, 'you gotta do something, even though you know it's wrong!"

The arrangement is typical of the rest of the album, with plenty of horns and strings and a thumping slap-bass performance giving the track power. The vocals are excellent and Street and Leonard work well together, although it's a shame that, on future albums, this duo weren't utilised more. Yet, even their gallant efforts can't save the song from itself, a risqué number for the era, no doubt. All this combined to a flop when it was released as a single in September 1978, peaking at number 48 on the R&B chart and failing to chart at all on the pop chart.

'Ever Ready Love' (Harold Beatty, Brian Holland, Marcia Woods)
Easily the best song on *Bare Back*, 'Ever Ready Love' returned the group to the style of ballads that helped make them famous in the first place and that the group had yearned for in their later years at Motown. Leonard takes the lead and delivers one of his finest performances as a Temptation, his unique falsetto soaring across the more muted horn and string arrangement. Indeed, unlike other tracks on the album, the arrangement is more measured, making for a more pleasant listen; the horns and strings complement rather than dominate, allowing Leonard room to manoeuvre. Leonard recalled that 'the key was very high, but they [the Hollands] wanted an edge to the song. So, I went with their direction.'

Given the song's strength, Atlantic released it as the album's second single in November 1978, and although it, too, failed to break onto the pop chart, it did somewhat better on the R&B chart, peaking at number 31. Leonard loved the song so much that he later rerecorded it on his solo album *Then & Now*, but the original is far superior.

'Wake Up To Me' (Harold Beatty, Brian Holland, Marcia Woods)
Another decent ballad, 'Wake Up To Me' once again features Leonard on lead vocals, as well as an infectious mid-tempo groove, driven along by the bass

and layered with disco-influenced guitar playing, and a nice string arrangement from Riser that doesn't overpower the track. The song is lyrically similar to their earlier ballads, with a simple, romantic premise in which the narrator just wants to wake up next to his woman.

Here, Brian Holland keeps the arrangement simple. Leonard's vocals are a delight and the backing vocals are equally sweet, as is the saxophone solo after the second chorus. While the saxophone wails, The Temptations sing the line 'wake up to me baby, wake up', which proves catchy on repeated listening. It's not quite enough to save *Bare Back*, but it's certainly one of the few better tracks from their time at Atlantic Records.

'You're So Easy To Love' (Harold Beatty, Brian Holland, Marci Woods)
'Wake Up To Me' segues into 'You're So Easy To Love', with Franklin taking the lead from Leonard. According to Leonard, Franklin and he had been roommates on tour, and they wanted to reflect their bond on a record. Franklin begins where Leonard leaves off, with a spoken verse, wishing his woman 'good morning' and telling her how nice it is to wake up to her as she's 'so easy to love'.

The spoken-word introduction lasts nearly a minute before Franklin sings the first verse, and he lays the romance on thick, his deep bass vibrating through the track while the rest of the group sing some incredibly sweet harmonies as a counterpoint. The strings are equally saccharine, Riser outdoing himself to create a sentimental feel on the track, again counteracting the rumble of Franklin's vocals, creating one of the redeeming moments on *Bare Back*.

'I See My Child' (Benjamin Wright, Otis Williams, David English, Richard Street, Glenn Leonard)
The only song written by members of the group to be included on *Bare Back*, with longtime collaborator Benjamin Wright, it features a rare lead by Otis Williams, although one he shares with Price. On the face of it, the song sounds like a ballad, but the lyrics tell the story of a painful divorce, with the narrator addressing their child caught in the middle of proceedings. Williams himself had gone through a divorce involving his son Otis Lamont Miles, which is presumably the basis for 'I See My Child'. Reading the lyrics, it's actually quite sad, especially the section where the narrator tells his son not to cry:

> Now go on
> Take Momma's hand, young man
> Don't cry run along
> Someday you might understand

The narrator even understands if his ex-wife finds someone new, but declares that his love for his child will never end. For Williams, this was certainly the case: tragically, his son was killed in a construction accident in 1985. Listening to 'I See My Child' with that knowledge makes it even more poignant.

'Touch Me Again' (Harold Beatty, Brian Holland, Eddie Holland)
Bare Back ends how it started with another fiery disco-jam. The first five seconds fool you into thinking another ballad is on its way before the song explodes with strings and horns and a thumping bassline. The song is standard disco fare, in which the narrator 'explodes' when his woman touches him, with Street singing the lead. Again, he's doing his best impression of Dennis Edwards, almost shouting the lyrics, although with less success than Edwards would have had. It's not a bad lead, and his workmanlike voice suits the disco-style track well.

Like the production on *Do The Temptations*, the Hollands threw all they had at 'Touch Me Again'. Eddie 'Bongo' Brown hits his instruments with intensity, matched by the unrelenting horn and string arrangement from Riser. Of all the disco-oriented tracks on *Bare Back*, this is probably the best, though whether longtime Temptation fans reached this final track on the album is anyone's guess.

Other Albums

Diana Ross & The Supremes Join The Temptations (1968)

What better way to drive sales than to pair Motown's two biggest acts on an album? Even better, at least for Motown, was the decision to record covers selected from their own Jobete publishing catalogue, meaning that no royalty payments would leave the company. As a result, there are versions of Smokey Robinson's 'I Second That Emotion', Marvin Gaye's 'Try It Baby' (featuring a rare lead from Melvin Franklin) and a lacklustre version of 'Ain't No Mountain High Enough', which, of course, Diana Ross revisited as a solo artist a few years later.

The highlight of the album, however, is a cover of 'I'm Gonna Make You Love Me', originally recorded by Dee Dee Warwick and written by Kenny Gamble, Leon Huff and Jerry Ross. Eddie Kendricks duets with Diana Ross, and it works perfectly; there's even a little spoken-word verse from Otis Williams in the bridge. Williams also gets a rare lead on the Burt Bacharach-Hal David classic, 'This Guy's In Love With You'. There's also another take on 'The Impossible Dream', which The Temptations recorded for *In A Mellow Mood.*

Unlike The Temptations, where their lead parts are shared around, Diana Ross, unsurprisingly, given her status at Motown and in the eye of the ever-watchful Berry Gordy, sings all the female leads here. And, like most of The Supremes' records at this point, the female vocals are augmented by Motown's in-house backing group, The Andantes. By this point, Mary Wilson and Cindy Birdsong (who replaced original Supreme Florence Ballad a year earlier) rarely appeared on their own albums. *Join The Temptations* is the first album on which Dennis Edwards appeared, his vocals hastily replacing those already recorded by David Ruffin. However, with this being another vehicle for Diana Ross, it's really all about her.

Diana Ross & The Supremes With The Temptations – The Original Soundtrack From TCB (1968)

Airing on 2 December 1968, *TCB* (a then-popular acronym for 'Taking Care Of Business', made famous by Elvis Presley) was a television special for the US television network NBC and saw Motown's two biggest groups perform together, trading songs and leads, but with Diana Ross very much at the centre of proceedings.

But as good as Ross and The Supremes were, they simply couldn't match the vocal firepower that The Temptations had to offer, and it shows on the soundtrack to *TCB*. The Temptations' harmonies are slicker, richer and more soulful than those The Supremes could offer, even if, of course, the real point of the show was to promote Diana Ross as Motown's biggest superstar.

As with both groups' previous live albums, the soundtrack has a mix of each groups' hits as well as standards, and for good measure, covers of non-Motown hits, such as 'Respect' and a medley of 'A Taste Of Honey', 'Eleanor

Rigby', 'Do You Know The Way To San Jose' and 'Mrs Robinson'. Both groups duet together and also perform solo, the highlight being 'For Once In My Life', a song that had become one of Paul Williams' leads in concert. The performance on *TCB* is superior to the studio version on *In A Mellow Mood* and the previous live version on *Live At The Copa* and *The Temptations Show*. Indeed, it's a gut-wrenching performance that almost brings Paul to tears. That performance alone makes *TCB* well worth a listen.

Together (1969)

Together follows where *Join The Temptations* left off, with more duets on mostly Motown classics. They take on Stevie Wonder's 'Uptight (Everything's Alright)', Marvin Gaye's 'I'll Be Doggone' and a medley of 'My Guy, My Girl' ('My Guy' was originally recorded by Mary Wells and 'My Girl' by The Temptations and both were written by Smokey Robinson) to create what Quint Kik of *AllMusic* described as 'creative poverty at its most exemplary.'

None of the covers exceed the original in quality or excitement and sound a little run-of-the-mill. The two groups do cover a few non-Motown songs as well, but again, none add much to the originals. Mary Wilson is given a rare lead alongside Eddie Kendricks on Frankie Valli's 'Can't Take My Eyes Off You', which is probably the highlight of the album. Wilson continued to sing this as her only lead in concert with The Supremes until Ross's departure in 1970. They also cover The Band's 'The Weight', which sees Ross sing the main lead along with contributions from Paul and Eddie – a misjudged cover perhaps as Ross's voice isn't strong enough for it to work (compared with the version The Staples Singers recorded, with Mavis Staples on lead). 'The Weight' was released as a US single but failed to chart.

The album itself sold reasonably well, hitting number 28 on the US albums chart. But, unlike *Join The Temptations*, there's very little worth returning to – it's a novelty record designed to shift units rather than develop either group's sound or credibility. Given that The Temptations had released the *Cloud Nine* album at the beginning of 1969, *Together* was, at least artistically, a step backwards. Considering the vocal talent on offer, it was a missed opportunity to do something truly incredible.

Along with *Join The Temptations*, *Together* was reissued in 2004 on the compilation *Joined Together: The Complete Studio Sessions*, including tracks recorded but not included on the album, including a frantic medley of early Supremes hits and a decent cover of another Bacharach-David standard, 'A House Is Not A Home'.

Diana Ross And The Supremes* & The Temptations – On Broadway (Original TV Sound Track) (1969)

After the success of the *TCB* special, it was inevitable that another TV special between the two groups would be filmed. Unlike *TCB*, the soundtrack album has yet to be released digitally. The TV special and resulting album follow the pattern set by *TCB*, with the show originally titled 'G.I.T On Broadway' ('G.I.T' standing for 'Gettin' It Together'). As the title suggests, the special is reliant on show tunes, including a selection of Broadway songs presented in a medley and a song from *Fiddler On The Roof*. It does include a performance of 'Funky Broadway', which had first appeared on *Join The Temptations*. It's not as fun or enjoyable as *TCB*, one only for the most devoted of Supremes or Temptations fans.

The Temptations' Christmas Card (1970)

In the middle of Whitfield's psychedelic soul period, The Temptations still managed to record their first Christmas album, released in October 1970, their fourth album that year (*Psychedelic Shack* came out in March, *Live At London's Talk Of The Town* in July and *Greatest Hits II* in September). Whitfield, either too busy or not caring for such material, left the production up to Barrett Strong and Clay McMurry.

The album consists of classic Christmas fare, from a relaxed doo-wop influenced version of 'Rudolph The Red-Nosed Reindeer' to a frantic version of 'Santa Claus Is Comin' To Town' and a beautiful version of 'White Christmas', featuring Kendricks and Paul Williams sharing the lead. There's also a version of 'Silent Night', which was eclipsed by their second version on *Give Love At Christmas*, released a decade later. There are plenty of jingle bells to set the Christmas scene, and the vocals are, as always, impressive. Everyone gets some lead to sing, even Otis Williams, who does a fine job on 'The Christmas Song'. Overall, it's a decent Christmas album, suited for romantic nights in, waiting for the big man to climb down the chimney.

Live Albums

Temptations Live! (1967)

This is the only live album that features the original 'Classic Five' Temptations of Eddie, Paul, David, Otis and Melvin. The album was recorded during a performance at Detroit's hip nightclub The Roostertail. Motown's acts were regularly booked there throughout 1966 as part of a 'Motown Mondays' promotion, where each Monday, a different act from the label would perform. These performances spawned live albums from not only The Temptations but also Junior Walker & The All-Stars and Martha Reeves & The Vandellas (The Supremes' recording from the Roostertail came out on the expanded *I Hear A Symphony* album in 2012).

Unlike The Temptations' later performances at the Copa, this set is primarily focused on their then-current hits, with a couple of covers thrown in for good measure, including David Ruffin singing an excellent version of 'Yesterday'. It's a thrilling performance – although, of course, you can't experience the slick choreography the group had become known for – with everyone bar Otis having a turn singing lead. Melvin Franklin thrills with his version of 'Old Man River', Paul sings an extended version of 'Don't Look Back' (which the crowd sing the chorus back to him) and Eddie glides through 'Get Ready', 'The Way You Do The Things You Do' and a fast opening medley of early hits. But it's David Ruffin who truly shines, a singer at his peak, but, of course, by this point in the group's history, his time as a Temptation was running short.

Live At The Copa (1968)

Recorded at New York's Copacabana supper club, *Live At The Copa* was the first Temptations album to feature Dennis Edwards as lead singer. Unlike *Temptations Live!*, the setlist mixes hits with standards from their *In A Mellow Mood* album, an approach Berry Gordy took with The Supremes during their performances at the club. Side one features some of their big hitters – 'Get Ready', 'You're My Everything' and 'I Wish It Would Rain' – whereas side two is dominated by standards and selections from *In A Mellow Mood*, including a rendition of Gershwin's 'Swanee' (which was not recorded as part of *In A Mellow Mood*).

The highlight of the set, though, is Paul Williams' live rendition of 'For Once In My Life', although he improved on it on the *TCB* TV soundtrack with Diana Ross & The Supremes, released the same year. But it's Edwards who perhaps impresses most on *Live At The Copa*. If he was nervous during these early performances with the group, it doesn't show; instead, he makes an impressive debut as a Temptation, handling Ruffin's material with ease while also making it his own.

The Temptations Show (The TV Soundtrack) (1968)

One of Motown's promotional tactics was to produce special television programmes. They introduced acts to mainstream American audiences, and the costs of producing the show could be offset by syndication across the country and by releasing the soundtracks as albums. The setlist of *The Temptations Show* follows in a similar vein to their performances at the Copa, mixing both hits along with standards. Here, the group rattle through a long medley of hits, a full rendition of 'Cloud Nine' and 'Runaway Child, Running Wild', alongside standards such as 'Ol' Man River'. There's even a 'comedy routine' that features 'Hello Young Lovers', covered on the *In A Mellow Mood* album, 'Cloud Nine' again and 'If I Didn't Care'.

The arrangements are brassy and the horns dominate, and there are also contributions from actor and comedian George Kirby and actor Kaye Stevens. It's not as good as other live efforts from the group, but an interesting artefact from a pivotal moment in the group's career.

Live At London's Talk Of The Town (1970)

Recorded at London's famed 'Talk of the Town' nightclub, this album features a more settled Dennis Edwards than on *Live At The Copa*: in the years prior, he had firmly established himself as the group's lead singer, and The Tempts had even won their first Grammy for 'Cloud Nine'. Of course, storm clouds were on the horizon for the group with the upcoming departures of Eddie Kendricks and Paul Williams, but both are present here and deliver some excellent performances. The album opens with a nearly nine-minute-long medley of some of their earlier (and biggest) hits, including 'My Girl', 'Get Ready' and 'Ain't Too Proud To Beg'. Whoever arranged the medley, presumably their guitarist and musical director, Cornelius Grant, did an excellent job.

Live At London's Talk Of The Town essentially defined The Temptations' live sound for decades to come. Backed by Burt Rhodes and his orchestra (although it's just horns) and their usual touring rhythm section, they recreate the Motown Sound pretty authentically. Vocally, the group had rarely sounded better, managing the frantic pace of the opening medley with ease, and excelling on the slower numbers.

Like most of Motown's live albums, it's a mix of standards, covers and hits: Paul Williams sings Sammy Davis Jr's 'I Gotta Be Me', Dennis Edwards sings 'The Impossible Dream', while Eddie Kendricks puts his own stamp on 'Love Theme From Romeo And Juliet'. Even Otis Williams gets a short lead, singing a snippet of the Bacharach-Davis classic 'This Girl's In Love With Me', which they had previously recorded with Diana Ross & The Supremes. A group truly at their peak, but one with a lineup which was sadly not destined to last.

In Japan (1974)

Released initially only in Japan, this excellent live album was finally reissued by Hip-O Select in 2004 as a limited edition CD and is now available to download and stream. Incredibly, given their non-stop touring schedule, this is the last official Temptations live album to be released featuring the post-

Eddie Kendricks and Paul Williams lineup of Otis Williams, Melvin Franklin, Dennis Edwards, Richard Street and Damon Harris. At this point, the group had not simply reverted to playing the hits in concert, as they would do later; instead, the album is heavy on the group's more recent recordings, such as 'Plastic Man' and 'Hey Girl (I Like Your Style)'. Led by longtime Temptations guitarist Cornelius Grant, the rhythm section do a remarkable job replicating the songs live, aided by a bold horn section. The mix is heavy on the bottom, with the bass at times being overwhelming in the mix.

Given the personnel changes, though, the group sound invigorated and the harmonies are tight; Damon Harris does a great job on 'Just My Imagination (Running Away With Me)', and Dennis Edwards leads the line with fiery performances of 'Cloud Nine' and 'Papa Was A Rolling Stone', the album's highlight.

Epilogue

With the disappointing chart performance of *Bare Back*, The Temptations had begun to realise that leaving Motown might have been a mistake after all, as had letting Dennis Edwards leave the group. Louis Price was a gifted vocalist, but he struggled to cement his position in the group, not helped by the weak material he was forced to work with (indeed, it's arguable whether Edwards could have done any better).

Interestingly, though, a third album of material was recorded for Atlantic, but, presumably, after *Bare Back* flopped, Atlantic shelved it. Williams wrote later that he felt it was their best material of the Atlantic period, but so far at least, none of the material has been released and is still in the Atlantic vault – but it's unlikely it'll ever be released. Atlantic, though, decided to cut their losses, and in 1979, they released The Temptations from their contract, and once again, they were looking for a new deal.

Leaving Motown had certainly been a gamble, but at the time, the group no doubt felt it was the right one to take. But their brief tenure at Atlantic was neither the creative nor commercial success they craved, nor did they have any more involvement in writing or producing the material than they did at Motown. If anything, it suggested to Williams and Franklin that maybe Motown did know how to handle The Temptations after all. They initially spoke with the likes of Polydor, Warner Brothers and Philadelphia International Records (Kenny Gamble, one half of the Gamble-Huff production duo, was friends with Otis Williams), but no deal was forthcoming. After all, The Temptations were now essentially an oldies act and, of course, this lineup was not the original one, nor did it feature Dennis Edwards.

Luckily for The Temptations, though, both Berry Gordy and Smokey Robinson were keen to have the group back at Motown, even if some of the other company executives saw them as the label's past, not its future. Initially, the group, Williams in particular, were cautious about any return to Motown, but with few other options available, in 1980, The Temptations returned to Motown. Dennis Edwards was also brought back into the fold, while Price was let go to make way for his return. The Temptations were back home.